D1550491

SECONDARY ANALYSIS OF SURVEY DATA

K. JILL KIECOLT
LAURA E. NATHAN

Series: Quantitative Applications
in the Social Sciences

 a SAGE **UNIVERSITY** PAPER

53

SAGE **UNIVERSITY** PAPERS

Series: Quantitative Applications
in the Social Sciences

Series Editors: **John L. Sullivan,** *University of Minnesota*
Richard G. Niemi, *University of Rochester*

Editorial Consultants

Christopher H. Achen, *University of Chicago*
Peter M. Bentler, *University of California, Los Angeles*
Alan B. Forsythe, *University of California, Los Angeles*
David Knoke, *Indiana University*
Kenneth Land, *University of Texas*
Michael S. Lewis-Beck, *University of Iowa*
Forrest Nelson, *University of Iowa*
Richard Shavelson, *Rand Corporation*
Robert M. Thorndike, *Western Washington University*
Sanford Weisberg, *University of Minnesota*
Douglas A. Zahn, *Florida State University*

Publisher

Sara Miller McCune, Sage Publications, Inc.

Series / Number 07-053

SECONDARY ANALYSIS OF SURVEY DATA

K. JILL KIECOLT
Louisiana State University

LAURA E. NATHAN
Mills College

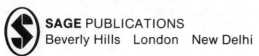
SAGE PUBLICATIONS
Beverly Hills   London   New Delhi

For information address:

SAGE Publications, Inc.
275 South Beverly Drive
Beverly Hills, California 90212

SAGE Publications India Pvt. Ltd.
M-32 Market
Greater Kailash I
New Delhi 110 048, India

SAGE Publications Ltd
28 Banner Street
London EC1Y 8QE
England

International Standard Book Number 0-8039-2302-3

Library of Congress Catalog Card No. 85-062111

SECOND PRINTING, 1987

When citing a University paper, please use the proper form. Remember to cite the correct
Sage University Paper series title and include the paper number. One of the following
formats can be adapted (depending on the style manual used):

(1) IVERSEN, GUDMUND R. and NORPOTH, HELMUT (1976) "Analysis of
Variance." Sage University Paper series on Quantitative Applications in the Social
Sciences, 07-001. Beverly Hills: Sage Pubns.

OR

(2) Iversen, Gudmund R. and Norpoth, Helmut. 1976. *Analysis of Variance.* Sage
University Paper series on Quantitative Applications in the Social Sciences, series no.
07-001. Beverly Hills: Sage Pubns.

CONTENTS

Preface

This monograph presents information on the use of precollected survey data in social research. The wide range of computer software packages and multivariate statistical techniques for data analysis have increased the utility of large-scale survey data sets for purposes other than those originally intended. Thus the emerging importance of so-called secondary analysis cannot be denied.

When it comes to understanding the organization of data archives and the subtleties of conducting secondary analysis, there is no substitute for experience. In this light, we were fortunate in having the help of many people while preparing our manuscript. Social science data archivists around the world responded to our letters and phone calls. Two archivists in particular, Ilona Einowski of the State Data Program in Berkeley, California, and Elizabeth Stephenson of the Data Archives Library at the University of California, Los Angeles, contributed enormously to our understanding of the variety and complexity of data archives. A number of social scientists also contributed generously to this work by sharing with us their successes and frustrations in working with preexisting data. We would like to thank Glen H. Elder, Jr., Howard E. Freeman, Mark Fossett, Norval D. Glenn, Herbert H. Hyman, Ronald C. Kessler, Douglas Longshore, Hart M. Nelsen, Linda B. Nilson, T. Wayne Parent, Patricia A. Roos, Marnie L. Sayles, Tom W. Smith, Nancy Thornborrow, Ronald E. Weber, Frederick D. Weil, and Michael J. White. We appreciate the willingness of these investigators to provide accounts of their experiences with secondary analysis. We would also like to thank Rae R. Newton, Richard G. Niemi, and two anonymous reviewers for helpful comments on an earlier draft.

The order of authorship is strictly alphabetical. The entire work is a collaborative effort.

5

Series Editor's Introduction

Secondary analysis of survey data, comprising a set of research techniques that make use of existing surveys, has recently assumed a central position in social science research. Nevertheless, no major American publication on secondary analysis has appeared since Herbert Hyman's *Secondary Analysis of Sample Surveys* (1972). Since then, social science data archives have proliferated, and existing survey data and statistical computing programs have become increasingly available. These developments have created a need for the kind of volume presented here. In *Secondary Analysis of Survey Data*, Jill Kiecolt and Laura Nathan have put together a highly readable text identifying the advantages and limitations of secondary analysis and detailing strategies for locating and making effective use of existing survey data.

Chapter 2 contains information on how to identify appropriate data for secondary use. It begins by outlining an overall approach to finding relevant data. In order to convey a sense of the variety of data files held, functions served, and procedures followed by social science data archives, a few major archives are described in detail: the Inter-University Consortium for Political and Social Research, the Social Science Research Council Data Archive, the Steinmetz Archives (Amsterdam), the Roper Center for Public Opinion Research, and the Louis Harris Data Center. An important feature of this chapter is a table identifying additional major public access archives in the United States. Complete names, addresses, and phone numbers of data archives both within and outside the United States are provided in two appendices. The chapter also profiles several major American data series, including the General Social Survey, the Census Public Use Microdata Sample, and the American National Election Study.

Chapter 3 offers both caveats and guidelines for conducting secondary analysis. It raises several problems that researchers may encounter, along with solutions using illustrations drawn from published research. New students will find valuable information here, but so too may experienced secondary analysts who have not kept up with some of the more recent developments regarding sample comparability, pooling samples, calculating significance tests using multiple samples, and so on.

Researchers of all social science disciplines in both academic and applied settings will find this text extremely useful. The chapter on locating data provides practical information for all secondary analysts, from advanced undergraduates to seasoned researchers. The chapter on making effective use of data introduces analysis problems that all secondary users confront at one time or another. While making complete use of the solutions proposed may require additional reading and more statistical training than some readers will have, the material is presented in a manner that will provide all readers with a clear understanding of how to approach previously collected survey material. This dual emphasis makes *Secondary Analysis of Survey Data* the most valuable guide to the secondary analysis of survey data to have come along in recent years.

—Richard G. Niemi
Series Co-Editor

SECONDARY ANALYSIS OF SURVEY DATA

K. JILL KIECOLT
Louisiana State University

LAURA E. NATHAN
Mills College

1. INTRODUCTION

The method of data collection known as survey research has for some time been central to investigation in the social sciences. The survey is a rather flexible tool, and survey research easily lends itself to the exploration of a wide range of topics requiring different types of data (demographic, attitudinal, behavioral, and so on). The role of survey research will undoubtedly be enlarged by the availability of large-scale social surveys which can be used for a variety of research projects in addition to the ones for which they were originally intended.

Traditionally, social scientists have been encouraged to collect their own data, regardless of the data collection method used. After selecting the question to be addressed, researchers are charged with designing their research in keeping with the problem at hand. When survey research is the method of choice, questions can be developed to elicit precisely those data that are needed.

Unfortunately, independent data collection by the individual investigator has become increasingly difficult. Constraints of the current economic climate and declining resources for research in the social sciences have made it necessary for more researchers to rely on existing survey data. The potential for accomplishing original research with precollected data is nonetheless tremendous. Further, inasmuch as original data cannot be gathered for times past, analysts of change must rely on existing data to probe shifts in attitudes and behavior. Secondary analysis is thus gaining a central role in contemporary social research.

9

This type of analysis is neither a specific regimen of analytic procedures nor a statistical technique. Rather, it is a set of research endeavors that use existing materials. It differs from primary research in that primary analysis involves both data collection and analysis, while secondary analysis requires the application of creative analytical techniques to data that have been amassed by others.

"Meta-analysis," or "quantitative literature review," should be differentiated from the secondary analysis of documents or surveys. Meta-analysis integrates the findings from a universe (or sample) of investigations of some phenomenon. That is, the study itself becomes the unit of analysis. Meta-analysis involves using published research results to compute an overall level of significance for an array of comparable test statistics, such as correlations or t values (see Rosenthal, 1984, for a review of methods). It can also be used to find the average effect size of a treatment across studies—for example, the mean difference in outcomes between control groups and groups receiving therapy (Glass, 1978). Meta-analysis has been used primarily to evaluate experimental research in psychology and education, but the technique may also be applied to research in other disciplines.

Documents are written materials that contain information. They are rarely developed with social research in mind, yet they are potentially rich sources of information on social phenomena. Document studies are often qualitative, but they may also employ quantitative content analysis techniques. Since the researcher must construct the categories for analysis, determine the recording unit, and decide on the system of enumeration, even content analysis assumes a degree of subjectivity.[1]

Documents are used extensively in historical research and often provide data over time where no similar data exist. While documents themselves may be classified as primary (i.e., eyewitness descriptions of behavior or events) or secondary (i.e., second-hand accounts), document studies are virtually always secondary analyses. Documents are used less frequently, however, than surveys for secondary analysis.

Surveys have been employed to elicit information on a wide variety of topics from both general and specialized populations. There is now an abundance of surveys on population characteristics, attitudes, and behavior. Secondary analysis of existing surveys allows researchers access to data from large, national samples—data that would be difficult for a lone researcher to gather. Both large and more specialized archives have been established that typically make surveys available for a modest fee (see Chapter 2). Technological advances, such as the effective storage of data in machine-readable form and the availability of statistical computing programs, as well as widespread researcher access to computers, have also contributed to the popularity of using precollected survey data for original research. As a consequence, secondary analysis of survey data is likely to maintain a dominant position in social science research for the foreseeable future.

Advantages of Secondary Survey Analysis

The primary advantage of secondary survey analysis is its potential for resource savings. Secondary research requires less money, less time, and fewer personnel and is therefore attractive in times of economic fluctuations, when the funds available for research are limited or uncertain. With data already collected, the costs are only those of obtaining the data, preparing them for analysis (such as ensuring that all data are computer-ready and compatible with the system), and conducting the analysis (buying computer time, and so on). Compared with the time normally required to collect data in social research, the time necessary for acquiring an appropriate data set is miniscule. Further, a researcher can complete a research project independently, thereby eliminating the need for ancillary research staff. Secondary analysis also obviates the need for researchers to affiliate with a large organization in order to command the backing necessary for acquiring adequate survey data.

Another advantage is that secondary analysis circumvents data collection problems. Data archives furnish a large quantity of machine-readable survey data spanning many topics, time periods, and countries (see Chapter 2). Many available data sets provide the benefits of nationally representative samples, standard items, and standard indices. Both data availability and improvements in technology facilitate research. Growing numbers of researchers have access to computer facilities and computer software packages such as SPSS[x] (1983) and SAS (1982) to simplify analysis.

A variety of research projects can be accomplished with precollected data. When used in exploratory research prior to fielding a new survey, secondary analysis can uncover aspects of a research problem that require elaboration, groups that need to be oversampled, grounds for hypothesis revision, and the need to refine and improve existing measures (Hyman, 1972). Secondary analysis may be employed for a variety of research designs, including trend, cohort, time-series, and comparative studies (see Chapter 3). Existing data can also be combined with other types of data to investigate a problem more thoroughly. For example, they can be combined with primary data to render an analysis dynamic, or they can be used to supplement in-depth interviews. Demographic and historical studies and research conducted under time constraints, such as policy-related projects, often require the use of existing data.

Our increased familiarity with and use of preexisting data encourage social scientific progress. Data sets such as the General Social Survey and the American National Election Study are widely used, and investigators who employ these data sets can turn to other researchers with questions on data handling. The widespread use of particular data sets also allows authors greater ease of reporting. On the basis of earlier articles which have used or discussed a particular data set, most readers will be familiar with relevant aspects of the survey such as the sampling procedure and question wording.

Familiarity with existing databases also offers researchers the opportunity to build on what is available and conduct trend studies. For example, to study trends in the enjoyment of work, Glenn and Weaver (1982) commissioned the inclusion of some work enjoyment questions on the 1980 Gallup national survey which duplicated items that had not been asked since 1955. Finally, the better acquainted researchers become with existing databases, the greater the potential for creative new research. Ideas for studies often emerge from interaction between a researcher's substantive interests and his or her intimate knowledge of information contained in data files.[2]

Limitations of Secondary Analysis

Although the advantages of secondary analysis clearly outweigh the disadvantages, there are limitations. Many of the problems that secondary analysts encounter are intrinsic to the survey method, but some are unique to secondary analysis. A major problem is data availability. Despite the development of data archives, researchers sometimes have trouble locating what they need. Some topics lend themselves more readily to secondary analysis than others; for example, researchers interested in drug abuse, crime, and physical health are likely to have an easy time finding data. In more specialized areas, such as mental health epidemiology, however, there are relatively few publicly available databases, and investigators must depend on the generosity of individuals who own private data files. Often primary researchers are reluctant to share their data, as reputations are made by publishing work from a controlled body of data. A different sort of data availability problem stems from a major mismatch of primary and secondary research objectives. Sometimes when information on specific items or individuals is desired, data are available only in scaled or aggregated form.

Some secondary analysts complain about the time involved in acquiring data sets from archives. While admittedly it often takes several weeks to obtain data, this time is short compared to the time it takes to design a survey and collect data. The situation is analogous to that of adoptive parents a decade or two ago. Many bemoaned the four- to six-month wait involved in adopting a child, despite the fact that it would take nine months to produce their own.

In order for a data set to be usable, researchers must know exactly what they are analyzing. Without complete and accurate documentation of all data on a file, it is difficult or impossible to locate needed information. Inadequate documentation sometimes occurs with data tapes produced by small research firms on a contract basis, but it is not usually a problem with data sets produced by large academic organizations. Major archives usually provide complete data documentation in a codebook that sequentially lists the variables in a data file, as well as describing them and their assigned values. Whenever possible, data files should be checked by comparing the marginal distributions of a subset of the variables with those reported by the original investigators.

Errors made in original surveys often are no longer visible, and it is impossible to differentiate interviewing, coding, and keypunching errors. Moreover, the survey procedures that were followed may not have been sufficiently documented to enable secondary analysts to appraise errors in data. Trivial sources of error, such as that from sampling design, may be magnified when a survey is put to other than its original use, and such errors may be compounded by combining surveys. For example, a study using a national sample that excludes the institutionalized population could draw misleading conclusions about very young or very old adults because of the relatively high proportions of these groups who reside in various institutions (Hyman, 1972). The problem would be compounded by using such samples for a trend study of old or young adults to the extent that the proportions of these groups in institutions have changed over time.

A related problem occurs when a secondary researcher wants to study a specific subpopulation but has only a broad-based, nationally representative sample. Unless the sample is enormous, there may be too few cases to conduct the desired statistical analysis. In such cases, pooling surveys for data on rare populations is a possibility (see Chapter 3).

Data quality is another reason that some researchers are leery of secondary research. Data files from surveys employing nationally representative samples, properly designed questionnaires, and rigorous procedures for interviewing and coding do not always exist. Even surveys of high quality may have measurement problems. Invalidity is of concern to the extent that survey items are imprecise measures of the concepts a secondary analyst has in mind, or that the variables have been poorly operationalized. Surveys rarely contain all the variables of interest to the secondary researcher, and even when they do there may be too few indicators of a concept for reliable measurement. Thus researchers sometimes need to use a number of surveys to assemble arguments that cannot be developed with the data from one survey alone. Using multiple surveys compounds potential error, however, and issues of comparability arise when measures of a concept are not strictly equivalent. In sum, secondary analysts must frequently make do with measures that are not precisely those desired. Often this results in criticism from peers for lacking hypothetically perfect indicators, or for proceeding atheoretically with research.

Another disadvantage of secondary analysis is the possible inhibition of creativity. If researchers use the same data sets repeatedly and are limited by the variables contained therein, scientific progress will be thwarted to some extent. More globally, continued use of the same indices and data sets may limit the scope of social science research. However, we believe that the inclusion of the same measures is necessary to ensure comparability. As long as new items are continually incorporated into surveys, advances will be made in the social sciences.

The increased availability of good survey data for secondary analysis is something of a mixed blessing to the degree that it has contributed to so-called "trendy" social research. That is, some researchers obtain a data set, apply a currently popular statistical technique, and then look for a problem to investigate. Without theory, however, the utility of social research is called into question. The proliferation of survey data for secondary analysis offers tremendous opportunity, but the "data set in search of analysis" approach yields only trivial findings.

2. LOCATING APPROPRIATE DATA

In defining research problems, some secondary analysts generate ideas and then search for appropriate data, while others browse through codebooks for inspiration. While both strategies are sometimes employed, a third, even more productive approach to generating ideas for research, as described in Chapter 1, involves a merging of one's general substantive interests and familiarity with existing data files. Ideas for research projects are usually influenced by one's knowledge of existing data. Prospective users often learn about the existence of pertinent data through sharing information with other researchers about data sets that bear upon their mutual interests, or through journal articles that cite data sources in the text or accompanying tables.

In the past, secondary analysts usually had to depend on identifying primary researchers who were willing to share their data, while today most secondary analysts obtain surveys from academic archives. During the late 1950s, about 20 years after the initial proliferation of surveys, data began to be systematically preserved and stored. Social scientists throughout the world recognized the broad research potential of these surveys, and with financial support from such agencies as the National Science Foundation (Geda, 1978), they worked to create archives to house and distribute machine-readable social data.

Social Science Data Archives

Social science data archives vary considerably in terms of source and level of funding. The better the funding, the greater the depth and breadth of the services provided by the archive. External funding (from agencies and foundations) has been central to the development and support of data archives, as archives typically charge only enough to cover the costs of their services. The current state of the economy and recent cutbacks in funding for education and research have slowed the development of many social science data archives. Hence some archives charge membership fees to other institutions to help maintain archive quality.

Archive size and extent of services are directly related to the level of funding. Some archives have rather limited holdings (a few major data sets or only those data sets generated by individuals who are affiliated with the larger institution), while others have literally thousands of data files. The extent of services generally increases with size.

The main service that social science data archives provide is the distribution (by loan or purchase) of machine-readable data files and accompanying documentation. Data are virtually always furnished on magnetic tape, but some data files are available on cards for users who have access only to older equipment. While some (typically smaller) archives supply only data and documentation for specifically requested data files, larger archives usually offer data search assistance. Many furnish information on data files held by other archives, and some locate and purchase data files for users.

Archive services are often directed toward aiding analysis once the data have been located. Many archives furnish technical assistance in the use of machine-readable data files. Others also perform customized data file extraction/tabulations that may be less expensive for a researcher than acquiring an entire data set, and that may eliminate a great deal of non-analytic work on a project. Some archives also offer statistical assistance.

Various archives sponsor direct educational activities, such as seminars and institutes (for example, the summer institute at the Inter-University Consortium for Political and Social Research). Many of these demonstrate how to prepare and work effectively with existing machine-readable data files. They may also address statistical applications for data analysis.

All archives acquire and store data, but they differ a great deal in data processing and the ability to prepare user-ready data files. A number of archives process data collected by researchers in the parent institution, putting them into machine-readable form and making them available to the user community. A few archives seek and/or accept data collected by external researchers, but only if the data do not require excessive "cleaning" (i.e., correcting for invalid codes) and documentation by archive staff.

Access to data and services also varies among archives. Some (usually very small) archives serve only individuals affiliated with the parent institution. At the other end of the spectrum are those that allow public access to all holdings (most archives have a few access restrictions). Some archives cater primarily to the parent institution's research community but serve the community at large with census and other government data files mandated for the public domain. Some maintain membership in the ICPSR and also have publicly available holdings. These archives make their files available to anyone but restrict access to ICPSR holdings to researchers affiliated with the member institution.

Social science data archives differ with respect to the special emphasis of their holdings and the location of the archive. For example, some archives specialize in economic data, others in health data, and still others in data on social and political attitudes. Most university-based social science archives are located in research centers on campus, but they can also be found in computer centers or libraries.

To gather more information on specific social science archives, researchers need only write directly to the archivists at selected institutions. Most archives have catalogues, available for a small fee (usually about $15), that describe archive services and holdings. Archives that do not publish catalogues usually have either holdings lists or general information brochures. Many archives also publish newsletters that provide updates on archive services and recent data acquisitions.

Appendices A and B provide listings of currently operational data archives within and outside the United States. In addition, each February issue of *American Demographics* includes a "Directory of Commercial Data Suppliers."

Searching for an Appropriate Data Set

Researchers who are considering the use of precollected survey data but who do not have a particular data set in mind should generally contact several archives in order to cast as wide a net as possible in searching for data sets that will fill their needs. For researchers who are familiar with the substantive emphases of various archives, a useful strategy is to approach those whose focus suggests that they will have suitable holdings.

The procurement of data generally requires at least two (and often three or more) correspondences with data archive staff. Researchers need to provide as much information as possible about the type of data they require. It is important, for example, to specify the population of interest. Respondents' race/ethnicity, age, sex, and country or region of residence are all factors that can potentially eliminate otherwise suitable data scts. The year(s) of interest also need to be specified. Further, the research design (i.e., whether the study will examine a phenomenon at one time, across time, or comparatively) must be noted. For example, if a trend analysis is to be conducted, multiple data sets with comparable items will be required. Because of the variability in charges for data files and data processing costs, researchers should also specify their budgetary constraints.

After requesting aid in identifying a suitable data set, the researcher will either be directed to an appropriate data file or asked for additional information until the most suitable data file is located. If the archive contacted has no relevant holdings, the researcher may be referred to other (sometimes non-academic) archives.

When an appropriate data set has been identified, the researcher may need to consult with computer personnel in order to provide archive staff with the technical specifications for the data tape, such as number of tracks, density, labeling, and so on. Once this information reaches the archive, it is typically only a short time before the researcher receives a tape.

Expanding the Search for Data

One last point is that any storehouse and supplier of data can be considered an archive. Given this notion, researchers should keep in mind alternatives to academic archives such as government agencies and other organizations. For example, the National Institute of Health and the Centers for Disease Control may have data on specific health or disease topics. Private research firms are also potentially rich data warehouses. These firms will often make available to researchers data from studies they have conducted and charge fees no higher than those requested by academic archives. Charitable organizations such as the American Cancer Society and commercial enterprises such as banks and insurance companies should also be considered viable data resources. Many companies have collected extensive information on special populations. An excellent example is the Ralston Purina Company, which has amassed more information on pet owners than any other organization. When seeking to acquire data from non-academic sources, researchers must make it clear that their goals will not conflict with the organization's objectives. Sometimes non-academic organizations will not allow direct access to their data but will perform retrieval procedures on specific research questions.

Despite the multitude of data resources, most secondary analysts rely on academic data archives to supply data files for the majority of their research projects. Descriptions of selected academic archives appear below. Although there are many archives throughout the world, those selected for extended comment were purposefully included here.

The Inter-University Consortium for Political and Social Research is the leading secondary survey data source for academic social science researchers. Many smaller archives are members of ICPSR, providing a large number of researchers easy access to the consortium's holdings. The Social Science Research Council (SSRC) Data Archive in England and the Steinmetz Archives in the Netherlands, two national social science data archives, serve as examples of the resources and services available from foreign data storehouses. The Roper and Harris Centers are major repositories of American public opinion data that have tremendous research potential. The following short descriptions convey a sense of the variety of data files held, the functions served, and the procedures followed by major social science data archives. In addition, Table 1 presents information on public access data archives with holdings of special interest to the social science community.[3]

Inter-University Consortium for Political and Social Research

The ICPSR, housed at the University of Michigan, is unique among social science data archives. Formed in 1962 as the Inter-University Consortium for Political Research, its purpose was to make survey data from the 1950s more widely available to researchers. The addition of the word "social" to the title more accurately reflects the current range of data available through the consortium. It is the world's largest repository and dissemination service for machine-readable social science data, housing over 17,000 computer-readable data files on contemporary and historical phenomena representing all social science disciplines and over 130 countries.

Frequently used American databases such as the American National Election Study, the U.S. Congressional Voting Records, the Panel Study of Income Dynamics (PSID), and the General Social Survey (GSS) are held by the ICPSR, as are many of the more important data sets generated by government agencies. National health studies, education studies, studies of consumer behavior, and employment studies are all available from the consortium. It also maintains numerous holdings from the Bureau of the Census, including the decennial census Public Use Microdata Samples (PUMS), the Current Population Survey (CPS) Annual Demographic Files from 1968 to 1983, and CPS supplements and special topic studies. Non-United States data files held by the ICPSR include election studies, as well as many "Euro-Barometers" (see, e.g., Rabier and Inglehart, 1975), the European community's cooperative public opinion surveys highlighting regional integration and the quality of life.

Two smaller archives operate under the auspices of the ICPSR. The National Archive of Computerized Data on Aging (NACDA) was developed by the consortium in collaboration with the Institute of Gerontology at the University of Michigan. This archive holds data files on topics related to aging such as health, decisions on retirement, causes of death, and stereotypes of aging. The Criminal Justice Archive and Information Network (CJAIN), supported by the Bureau of Justice

TABLE 1
Major Public Access Social Science Data Archives: Their Substantive Emphases and Services

Archive Name and Affiliation	Substantive Emphasis/Special Holdings	DD	IR	DA	CT	TA	SA	Data File Charges[b]	Catalog/Directory
California									
Project Talent Data Bank American Institutes for Research	Human development	yes	no	no	yes	yes	yes	$300 for the Public Use sample/custom files for $500 to $2000	yes
Rand Corporation Data Facility The Rand Corporation	Health, education, and census data/Housing Assistance Supply Experiment; County business patterns 1962-current	yes	yes	yes	sc[c]	sc	no	$100 per file + $15 per tape reel	yes, but outdated[d]
State Data Program University of California at Berkeley	Political and social attitudes/ the California polls	yes	yes	yes	yes	yes	yes	$85-$250	yes
Connecticut									
The Roper Center for Public Opinion Research The University of Connecticut	Political and social attitudes/ Gallup polls; Roper polls; major media polls (CBS, ABC, NBC, L.A. *Times*); Yankelovich, Skelly and White data	yes	yes	no	yes	no	sc	$115 per data set (non-ISLA)/$75 per data set (ISLA members)	yes[d]
Illinois									
National Opinion Research Center University of Chicago	General social science data/ Occupational Prestige studies; 1973-1974 continuous national survey emphasizing questions on energy	yes	yes	no	yes	yes	yes	$100 per study	yes[d]

Services[a]

	Holdings/Description							Cost	
Massachusetts									
The Henry A. Murray Research Center of Radcliffe College Radcliffe College	Women's lives	yes	yes	yes	yes	yes		$50	yes
Michigan									
Inter-University Consortium for Political and Social Research Institute for Social Research	Social and political data/many "special holdings" including the American National Election Studies, Roll Call Voting Records, Election Returns, National Crime Survey, Panel Study of Income Dynamics, the General Social Survey, and various census data. Special archives have been set up at ICPSR for aging and criminal justice data.	yes	yes	sc	sc	yes	yes	free to users at ICPSR member institutions/charges to others	yes
North Carolina									
The Louis Harris Data Center Institute for Research in Social Science	American social and political public opinion/The Harris Polls	yes	yes	yes	yes	yes	sc	$100 for first data file; $50 for each additional file	yes
Texas									
Drug Abuse Epidemiology Data Center Texas A & M University	Drug abuse	yes	no	no	no	sc	no	$100	yes
Virginia									
Data Use and Access Laboratories (DUALLABS)	Demographic and housing data/Family Growth Surveys, Annual Housing Surveys, and census data	yes	yes	yes	yes	yes	yes	$150 per reel of tape	no

(continued)

TABLE 1 Continued

Archive Name and Affiliation	Substantive Emphasis/ Special Holdings	Services[a]						Data File Charges[b]	Catalog/ Directory
		DD	IR	DA	CT	TA	SA		
National Technical Information Services	Data collected on grants made by the government; Department of Energy and National Center for Health Statistics data/newer energy and health tapes	yes	yes	no	sc	no	no	$460 per tape	yes
Washington, D.C.									
Data User Services Division Bureau of the Census	U.S. demographic and economic data/first archive to receive data collected by the Bureau of the Census	yes	yes	no	sc	sc	sc	$140	yes
Machine-Readable Records Branch (NNSR) National Archives and Records Administration	Federal records with extensive holdings in the areas of economics and finance, airline transportation, military records for the Vietnam conflict, education, health, international trade, international attitudes, civil rights, labor agriculture, and demographics	yes	sc	no	no	no	no	$104 per tape reel plus documentation charges	yes
Wisconsin									
Data and Program Library Service University of Wisconsin	Social and political data/early Current Population Surveys, Scientific Manpower Data	yes	yes	yes	no	yes	yes	$70-$120	yes

a. Key to services: DD: distribution of machine-readable data files and documentation; IR: information about data files held by other archives and referral to those archives; DA: location and acquisition of data held by other archives; CT: customized data tabulations; TA: technical assistance in the use of machine-readable data files; and ST: statistical assistance.
b. Charges for data files are highly variable. The amounts quoted here are "average" figures for the archives.
c. "sc" stands for special circumstances and indicates that this service is not typically performed for users.
d. Listing of data files only.

Statistics, was established in 1978 to encourage research in the fields of crime and criminal justice. Data from these specialized archives are acquired by following usual ICPSR procedures.

Archive activities are concentrated in three distinct areas. First, the consortium stores and disseminates machine-readable social science data deposited by scholars and purchased from commercial or governmental sources. Second, it trains scholars in empirical research through its summer program in Quantitative Methods of Social Research. Finally, the ICPSR provides advice and materials that facilitate the use of advanced computer technology.

Institutions of higher education that employ people working in the social sciences are eligible for membership in the ICPSR. Dues for each membership category are based on an institution's size and the type of social science program(s) offered. Federated and national memberships are available for groups of institutions. Yearly fees entitle a member institution's faculty and students access to the full range of consortium services through an official representative who serves as a liaison between users at that institution and ICPSR staff.

The consortium purchases major data sets that are likely to be used extensively by the social scientific community. Data files submitted to the ICPSR by other data centers or by individual researchers are accepted for storage, processing, and dissemination on the condition that they can be made available to requesters without restrictions. All data sets archived by the ICPSR are categorized as Class I, II, III, or IV according to the degree of processing attention they have received. Class I data have been checked, corrected, and formatted according to ICPSR specifications. Full codebook documentation accompanies Class I data. Class IV data and documentation are generally provided in their original form.

Both individuals affiliated with the consortium's member institutions and nonaffiliated researchers may use ICPSR data files. ICPSR data are obtained by completing an ICPSR Data Request Form or by writing a letter that specifies the requester's name, mailing address and phone number, the name and ICPSR study number of the desired data file, the medium of transmission (usually magnetic tape), and the specifications for preparing the tapes. Requests from individuals at member institutions are generally filled within two weeks, and charges for borrowing the data are covered by the institution's annual membership fee. Researchers not affiliated with a member institution are charged for data and must usually wait longer than two weeks for their requests to be filled. Documentation typically accompanies the data, but descriptions summarizing the contents of data files are available separately, either through the member institution's official representative or upon request.

Each year the ICPSR publishes its *Guide to Resources and Services*. The bulk of this publication is devoted to the archival holdings. Four sections in the catalogue are special indexes designed to help researchers find appropriate data: the ICPSR Study-Number Documentation Index, the Title-Documentation Index, the Principal Investigator Index, and the Subject Index. The first three indexes all give the study's catalogue number and title, as well as the catalogue page on which a brief study description appears. Documentation and cost information are also provided in the documentation indexes. The Study Number Index is arranged sequentially by ICPSR study number, and the Title and Principal Investigator Indexes are arranged alphabetically by title and principal investigator, respectively. The Subject Index has detailed subject terms (including geographical areas) arranged alphabetically and cross-referenced by ICPSR study numbers. Researchers interested in a particular subject can use the Subject Index in conjunction with the ICPSR Study Number-Documentation Index to locate pertinent study descriptions in the Archival Holdings section of the catalogue.

The part of the catalogue describing the ICPSR's archival holdings organizes studies into 17 broad subject areas (e.g., "Mass Political Behavior and Attitudes" and "Governmental Structures, Policies, and Capabilities"). Within each category, studies are arranged alphabetically by principal investigator or original data collector. An abstract and the "data class" of each study or study collection are provided. The catalogue also briefly describes the system of data classes (discussed earlier).

In addition to the annual *Guide to Resources and Services*, the consortium keeps members apprised of its holdings through a quarterly bulletin and a 24-hour hotline. The *ICPSR Bulletin* provides current information on existing and newly acquired data, ICPSR activities, and member institution activities. The hotline provides updates on acquisitions within existing data series. The hotline number is (313) 763-3486.

Social Science Research Council Data Archives

The Social Science Research Council (SSRC) Data Archive, established in 1967, is the largest existing repository of British social science data. The activities of the archive are supported by the Social Science

Research Council and by the University of Essex, where it is housed. The archive holds more than 1300 data sets from academic surveys, opinion polls, government studies, and market research projects and maintains a detailed, current record of British social surveys. In addition, it has catalogues of many other major data sets (both national and international) and will locate and acquire data for researchers. The archive has exchange relationships with a number of other major archives and is a member of the ICPSR, administering that organization's British national membership. It also belongs to the International Federation of Data Organizations (IFDO) and the International Association for Social Science Information Services and Technology (IASSIST).

To obtain data held by the SSRC Data Archive, a researcher need only fill out two forms. The first is an application form specifying one's complete requirements on codebook, data set, tape, and so on. The second is a User's Undertaking agreement indicating compliance with certain conditions for data use outlined by the archive. Data are supplied as blocked card images on magnetic tape in a format specified by the researcher. Copies of codebooks and original questionnaires are available at cost and may be examined before data are ordered.

The SSRC archive publishes two data catalogues—the *Guide to the Survey Archives Social Science Data Holdings and Allied Services* and an abbreviated guide for quick reference. The complete guide explains how to obtain data from and deposit data within the archive. It indexes data files on the basis of data depositor(s), survey title, study number, the geographic area studied, and the population of interest. For each holding, it gives the study number, access category (relating to restrictions imposed on data use by the depositor), data preparation category (indicating the amount of processing required to put data in perfect or near-perfect condition), the study's title and general purpose, a list of attitudinal/behavioral variables, a list of background variables, a list of directly related publications, the name(s) of the depositor(s), the sponsor(s) of the study, the study's principal investigator(s), sampling information (method, target sample, sample obtained, and the like), and the date(s) of the fieldwork. The catalogue classifies files according to 23 subject headings including social welfare, mass media studies, health services and medical care, economic behavior, and large-scale continuous and trend studies. The abbreviated catalogue employs the same subject headings for data set listings but has no index. Each entry gives the study number, the access and data preparation categories, the study's title and purpose, the name(s) of the depositor(s), and the study's location in the main catalogue.

The SSRC archive actively seeks to acquire new primary data files and, insofar as possible, processes data deposited by researchers. Depositors must complete a Depositor's Study Description Form outlining the study's purpose, time frame, sampling methods, and so on. The form also elicits information on the type of survey conducted, related publications, and the physical condition of the data. Depositors are allowed access to other archived data free of charge.

The tri-annual *Data Archive Bulletin* disseminates news about archive services and activities of interest to quantitative social science researchers. It lists new data file acquisitions of the SSRC archive according to topic heading and discusses some of these in detail. Periodically the bulletin publishes a specialized list of holdings in a particular field. It also announces conferences, fellowships, and data use training seminars, such as one-day workshops that bring together prospective users and researchers who have used certain types of data.

Steinmetz Archives

Named for Professor S. R. Steinmetz, one of the founders of sociology in the Netherlands, the Steinmetz Institute was established in Holland in 1964. The institute later became the archives, which are now part of the Social Science Information and Documentation Center (SWIDOC). The archives are dedicated to collecting, documenting, and distributing social science data for secondary analysis. They hold over 1200 data sets encompassing all of the social sciences. The studies vary in their nature and scope, but two particularly noteworthy items among the archives' extensive holdings are the Netherlands National Election Study and a series of over 700 weekly opinion polls conducted by the Netherlands Institute of Public Opinion and Marketing Research (NIPO) and dating from 1962. The NIPO polls include a number of standardized background variables and together have been documented and prepared for trend analysis.

The Steinmetz Archives routinely store data generated by several research institutes and by the government. Other files are purchased by the Archives based on information obtained through the report library of the SWIDOC and a selection of social science periodicals. The archives accept data sets from individuals and generally reimburse researchers for expenses incurred in preparing material for deposit. Studies stored at the archive need to have thorough documentation including a codebook, a copy of the questionnaire, two copies of a project report containing information on the study design, and a description of the tape format. In addition, depositors may stipulate restrictions on the use of their data.

The archives systematically classify each study in their *Catalogue and Guide* according to an international scheme that lists each study's identification number, title, data (year), keywords, themes, sampled universe, kind of data, substudies (associated with different themes), number of cases, number of variables, principal investigator(s), data depositor(s), access restrictions, and mode of storage. Catalogue indexes enable researchers to locate studies on the basis of keywords, study title, sampled universe, number of cases, study date, principal investigator, or data depositor.

The Steinmetz Archives offer many services to users, some free of charge. Their primary service is the distribution of archive data sets, along with accompanying documentation (codebooks and question-naires). Services offered without fee include the storage of data and documentation, consultation on research design and analysis, the acquisition of data and documentation from other archives (many foreign archive catalogues are available at the Steinmetz Archives), and the computer retrieval of study documentation. The archives' search system, the Remote Information Query System (RIQS), contains the study description and questionnaire text for each study held by the archives. Users may request a Profile Form on which they can specify the characteristics of the data they are seeking.

To obtain data held by the Steinmetz Archives, researchers must complete an application form which may be photocopied from the back of the Steinmetz Archives Catalogue. The application elicits infor-mation identifying the researcher, computer tape specifications, and the purpose for which the data set will be employed. Data are usually provided on magnetic tape as either card-image or SPSS files. Data set prices generally range from $15 to $100 per data file. At an additional charge, archive staff can convert data sets to nonstandard formats, create special data files for users, or perform data analysis.

Staff members are available to give invited lectures on the archives. They also provide training in data processing, the creation of special data files from archived material, and secondary analysis. The Steinmetz Archives do not currently publish a newsletter, but users are kept up to date on new acquisitions through a monthly list, *Titels van sociaalwetenschappelijk onderzoek*.

The Steinmetz Archives maintain close relationships with other European and American archives. They, along with the national archives of the German Federal Republic, Denmark, and the United Kingdom, are working to connect national computerized data files. The Steinmetz Archives hold memberships in the International Federation of Data Organizations(IFDO) and the International Association for Social Science Information Services and Technology (IASSIST). The archives also administer the Dutch National memberships in the European Consortium for Political Research (ECPR) and the ICPSR.

Major Poll Data Archives: The Roper Center for Public Opinion Research and the Louis Harris Data Center

Public opinion poll data are a rich resource for secondary analysis. Because they are either not held by or deemphasized by academic archives, researchers often overlook their potential. However, a number of survey organizations have conducted polls regularly for several decades, and the inclusion of repeated questions makes these data particularly useful for studying social change. Two major public access archives, the Roper Center for Public Opinion Research and the Louis Harris Data Center, are valuable storehouses of data collected by polling organizations.

Established in 1946, the Roper Center for Public Opinion Research has grown to become the largest public opinion data archive in the world. It is not, however, strictly a poll data archive, because some academic surveys, such as the General Social Survey (discussed below) are also held by Roper. Since 1977, the Roper Center has been housed at the Institute for Social Inquiry at the University of Connecticut, which operates it in cooperation with Williams College and Yale University. The center has more than 10,000 data files and adds approximately 500 new ones each year. The surveys span from the 1930s through the present and cover the United States and more than 70 foreign countries. Roper Center data files emphasize social values, social and political attitudes, policy preferences, and personal assessments.

Many survey organizations, such as the American Institute for Public Opinion (which conducts the Gallup polls), the Roper Organization, the

National Opinion Research Center, and Yankelovich, Skelly, and White, Inc. regularly contribute data files to the Roper Center. Many major media polls such as the ABC News/Washington *Post* polls, the NBC News/Associated Press polls, and the Los Angeles *Times* polls are also held by the Roper Center. Many studies of particular social scientific interest may be obtained from the Roper Center, including Samuel Stouffer's American Soldier Surveys from World War II, Alex Inkeles's "Becoming Modern" data from his project on the social and cultural aspects of development, the Virginia Slims American Women's Opinion Polls, a series of "State of the Nation" surveys, and a variety of American election polls. Data are typically supplied on 9-track magnetic tapes. OSIRIS files are also available for some widely used surveys. Researchers can acquire Roper data through User Services at the Center (see Appendix A).

Data may be obtained from the Roper Center either on an ad hoc basis or through the center's International Survey Library Association (ISLA) program, which offers memberships at three levels to colleges, universities, and nonprofit organizations. The annual membership fee provides these organizations with access to a specified number of data sets or equivalent services. Additional data sets and services are then available at a lower cost than that for nonmembers.

In addition to data set reproduction and distribution, the Roper Center performs customized tabulations and provides methodological and statistical assistance. Its computerized system offers customized search and retrieval, making it possible to locate items of interest through keywords and/or designated question wordings for specified time periods. For each question located, the system identifies the study, the population examined, and the responsible survey organization.

A number of publications and reference guides to Roper Center data are available. *Survey Data for Trend Analysis* (Southwick and Hastings, 1975) supplies information on repeated questions in the center's U.S. national surveys as far back as the 1930s. Although this volume is now out of print, public use libraries and data archives may have copies available for review. *A Guide to Roper Center Resources for the Study of American Race Relations* (Roper Center, 1982) identifies data files focusing on racial issues and lists more than 3000 questions in chronological order by topic. The *Roper Center American Collection* (Roper Center, 1984b) profiles the center's major U.S. holdings and briefly describes major survey organizations. Two publications apprise users of newly acquired data: *Data Acquisitions*, published in January and July, provides information on data sets obtained in the preceding six months, including the study name and Roper Archive Number, interview dates, the survey organization, and sampling information; *Data Set News* announces data files as they become available and provides summary descriptions of the subject matter addressed and the variables contained in each study.

The Louis Harris Center, established in 1965, is now part of the Social Science Data Library at the University of North Carolina, Chapel Hill. Louis Harris and Associates is a private international firm which since 1956 has conducted a variety of polls, including the continuing ABC News-Harris Survey. Harris offered to make available those polls that both Louis Harris and Associates and the University of North Carolina agreed were appropriate for the archive. In turn, the university is responsible for organizing, storing, and distributing the data (Presser, 1982).

The Louis Harris Center houses hundreds of Harris surveys covering such diverse topics as shifts in women's roles, taxation, elections, gun control, and buying intentions. Samples are drawn from special populations (e.g., physicians, trans-Atlantic travelers, and government and corporate leaders), from the voting population, or from the population at large. The general surveys are based on the adult, civilian, noninstitutionalized population of the continental United States. After the population has been initially stratified by geographic region and population density, multistage cluster samples are drawn from each stratum.

Data, accompanying documentation, and printed frequencies are available for $100 per file. When two or more data files are purchased simultaneously, the first file is $100 and each additional file is $50. A Request for Purchase form must be completed to obtain data, and it takes about three weeks for an order to be filled.

The Louis Harris Center provides all basic archive services. For $25, the archive will produce a complete set of frequencies for any data file, without requiring that a data tape be purchased. The center also performs custom data analyses. Perhaps most important, the Harris Center will search all general population Harris surveys for questions containing specified key words or phrases for a $30 charge. For the years 1963-1976, the question locator and retrieval system has been computerized. In addition to identifying and listing specific questions, the automated system provides information on "filter" questions (for more information on filters, see Chapter 3). For later surveys, the search is currently performed manually.

Several reference guides are available. The *Directory of Louis Harris Public Opinion Machine-Readable Data* (Institute for Research in Social Science, 1981) may be ordered from the Institute for Research in Social Science, Chapel Hill. A volume of brief descriptions of the Harris surveys and a set of abstracts with indexes are also available from the institute. The *Sourcebook of Harris National Surveys: Repeated Questions 1963-1976* (Martin et al., 1981) is useful for researchers planning trend studies. This volume indexes all social indicators found in the nearly 14,000 questions that have appeared in identical or slightly altered form in two or more Harris polls. Questions are classified according to 24 topics and various subtopics. This guide also discusses the Harris Center, the surveys, trend analysis with the surveys, and how to acquire data from the center. It may be purchased for $18 through the Institute for Research in Social Science, Chapel Hill.

The brief overviews of archives presented here give some indication of the many data sets available for secondary analysis. Data archivists at academic institutions can help direct researchers to an appropriate data file for a given research question. Furthermore, various directories, compendia, and archive catalogues and bulletins provide lists and/or summary descriptions of data files. Many government agencies have also compiled inventories of their data tapes. For example, the U.S. Census Bureau furnishes "U.S. Census Public Service Lists" for data that it has collected, the National Center for Education Statistics makes available its *Directory of Computer Data Tapes* (1981), and the U.S. Department of Commerce provides *Publications and Computer Tapes of the Bureau of Economic Analysis.* Journals such as the *Review of Public Data Use* occasionally publish specialized database inventories, such as those on "Health Surveys" (Mullner et al., 1983) and the "National Social Data Series" (Taeuber and Rockwell, 1982). The latter has been reprinted and circulated by the Social Science Research Council (SSRC) in Washington, D.C. SSRC committees have also assembled compendia of longitudinal data sets on "Middle and Old Age" (Migdal et al., 1981) and "Children and Adolescents" (Verdonik and Sherrod, 1984). "A Compendium of Academic Survey Studies of Elections Around the World" (de Guchteneire et al., 1985) appears in a recent issue of *Electoral Studies. The Sourcebook of Harris National Surveys: Repeated Questions 1963-1976* (Martin et al., 1981) provides information on questions duplicated over time in the Harris polls, and *Survey Data for Trend Analysis* (Southwick and Hastings, 1975) supplies an index to questions on U.S. surveys available from the Roper Center.

Major American Data Files

Below are brief descriptions of major American data sets. Each of these studies comprises a series that offers the potential for trend analysis. The General Social Survey, two Census Bureau surveys (the Public Use Microdata Samples of the decennial census and the Current Population Surveys), the American National Election Studies, the National Longitudinal Surveys of Labor Market Experience, the Panel Study of Income Dynamics, the Surveys of Consumers, and two health surveys (the National Health Interview Survey and the National Health and Nutrition Evaluation Survey) are described. These data series are widely applicable across social scientific disciplines but represent only the tip of the iceberg regarding data sets available for secondary analysis.

General Social Survey

The General Social Survey (GSS), conducted by the National Opinion Research Center (NORC) at the University of Chicago (Davis, 1983), is the first sociological survey designed particularly for secondary analysis (Glenn et al., 1978). Since data are not collected with a specific research project in mind, analyses employing the GSS do not constitute secondary research in the usual sense. However, the GSS has the advantages and pitfalls of any precollected survey data. From the beginning, the purpose of the GSS has been to provide social indicator data on a wide variety of attitudes, beliefs, and behavior. The data easily lend themselves to trend studies and replications because many of the items have been repeated across surveys, as shown in an appendix in the GSS codebook. The GSS has been conducted every year since 1972 (except 1979 and 1981) and is continuing annually. James A. Davis is the originator and principal investigator, and Tom W. Smith is co-principal investigator.

Each survey is a national cross-sectional sample of noninstitutionalized, English-speaking persons 18 years of age or older in the continental United States. A modified probability (block quota) sampling design was used from 1972 to 1974 and for half of the sample in the 1975 and 1976 surveys. Full probability sampling was used for the other half of the 1975 and 1976 surveys and for all subsequent surveys. The approximate sample size of each survey is 1500. The 1982 survey also contained a supplementary sample of 354 black respondents.

The GSS contains data on many topics, including stratification, Intrafamily relations, and morale. It also measures a plethora of attitudes on work, violence, sex roles, women's rights, abortion, and the civil liberties of racial and ethnic minorities, and contains indicators of personal happiness, job satisfaction, and confidence in institutions. General demographic data are collected, as are data on pre-adult, early adult, and adult background characteristics. Noteworthy pre- and early adult characteristics include parents' educational and job histories, parents' marital dissolution due to death or divorce, childhood family composition, religious background, and respondent's estimate of the family of origin's economic standing. Adult characteristics include age at first marriage, number of children born to the respondent, and respondent's marital history and military service. The GSS is suitable for investigating topics such as intergenerational mobility, the consequences of socialization experiences for adult behavior and beliefs, deviant behavior, and support for social movements.

Some items (e.g., basic demographic characteristics, happiness measures, and adolescent religious preferences) are included in every survey. Other items (such as attitudes toward violence and racial attitudes) follow a rotational scheme whereby data are collected on two out of every three surveys. More recently, the GSS design has been revised to allow intensive one-time coverage of given subjects. For example, the 1985 survey contains a battery of items on respondents' social networks.

Since 1977, cumulative GSS data files have been prepared which contain all data from the 1972 GSS through the most current survey, including survey supplements. The design of the GSS facilitates the study of social change through trend and cohort analyses. The cumulative data file structure also allows surveys containing equivalent items without a temporal dimension to be pooled for analysis (e.g., to obtain a larger sample of a small population), or to be treated as replications (see Chapter 3). The cumulative data files and accompanying documentation are available from the Roper Center or the ICPSR, and the NORC periodically publishes an annotated bibliography of papers that use the GSS (Smith, 1981a).

Census Bureau Data

The Bureau of the Census, an arm of the Department of Commerce, gathers more data than any other agency in the United States. Among its many tasks are the development and implementation of a variety of surveys. Although census data are designed for governmental purposes, they are rich resources for social scientists. In addition to individual and household data obtained through decennial censuses (discussed below), the bureau collects information on American agriculture, manufacturing, business and transportation, economics, geography, and state and local governments.

Copies of all census products for a given state (including microfiche, machine-readable data files, published volumes, and maps) are deposited in one of 44 state data centers operated in cooperation with state governments. These centers provide data from the Census Bureau, other federal agencies, and state sources. They also identify other organizations that are part of a state network for distributing data.

To inform researchers about census products and services available for purchase, the bureau publishes the *Bureau of the Census Catalog*. Additionally, the *Directory of Data Files* provides summaries of machine-readable data tapes available to users. A *Monthly Product Announcement* gives technical and price information about the latest census products. This listing is available free of charge from Data User Services (see Appendix A). Further information on data files mentioned in the *Monthly Product Announcement* can be obtained by requesting a Data Developments flyer for that file (also free of charge) from Data User Services. *Data User News*, published by the Bureau of the Census, is a monthly newsletter that describes census products, services, reference materials, conferences, and workshops. It costs $21 per year. The Data User Services' National Clearinghouse list for Census Data Services identifies all public and private organizations that distribute census products. *Telephone Contacts for Data Users*, compiled by the Bureau of the Census, lists various user services, general fields of interest, and specific topics within each field, together with the names and phone numbers of Census Bureau contacts. This listing also includes Census Bureau regional office and satellite office telephone numbers. As indicated earlier, the Bureau of the Census offers workshops, conferences, training courses, and seminars throughout the country to acquaint users with various activities, products, and services. These programs are advertised in *Data User News* and the *Monthly Product Announcement*.

Of the array of resources for social research that the Census Bureau offers, certain machine-readable data files are particularly suitable for social analysis. These are the Public Use Microdata Samples (PUMS) from the decennial census and the monthly Current Population Survey (CPS).

Public Use Microdata Samples

Since the first U.S. census in 1790, a census of the population has been conducted every ten years. The questionnaire has been modified after every decennial census, but most of the questions now included have been part of the survey since 1910 (Rowe, 1973). Questions are added to and deleted from the census questionnaire according to government data needs, and the final responsibility for census questions rests with Congress.

The decennial census of population and housing elicits self-report data on a variety of subjects. Basic demographic data and information on income and poverty are collected, and this survey is the source of most small area data on socioeconomic characteristics. Marital status has been ascertained since 1850, and some data on immigration have usually been collected.

In every decennial census, the bureau administers a longer version of the survey to a sample of the population. These longer questionnaires contain the items asked of all respondents plus additional social indicator questions. The Public Use Microdata Samples (PUMS) are representative samples drawn from these decennial census records. All questionnaire items except for identifying information (i.e., name and address) are available in the PUMS files. These files offer certain advantages over summary data tabulated by the Bureau of the Census. Individual-level data are more flexible than aggregate data, permitting a variety of cross-tabulations and multivariate analyses to be performed. Moreover, the large number of cases in the PUMS allows many special populations to be examined in detail. For example, researchers can study households with incomes below the poverty line, single parent households, widowed or divorced persons, or people working in the health industry.

The PUMS also have certain disadvantages. First, they are not available until about two or three years after data collection. Because of the large sample size, working with PUMS tapes can also be expensive. Finally, no small area analyses can be conducted; only large geographic units are included in PUMS so that individuals are not identifiable.

Public Use Microdata Samples for all decennial censuses from 1940 on are available on magnetic tape. The many repeated questions in these surveys offer the opportunity for trend analysis, but changes in the survey instrument present problems of comparability (see Glenn and

Frisbie, 1977; Martin, 1983; Chapter 3, this volume.) Also, the percentage of the population selected to fill out a more extensive questionnaire differs by census. In 1960, 25 percent of the population was sampled, and in 1980 over 19 percent. In 1970 there were two "long versions" of the instrument. In all, 5 percent of the population completed one version, and 15 percent the other.

Census PUMS may be used to address basic research questions as well as issues related to community action or social policy. Studies on poverty, the work force, mobility, marriage/fertility, and the characteristics of household members can all be conducted using the samples. Many quality-of-life measures can be constructed by combining variables. When census data by themselves are not adequate for testing proposed hypotheses, they can be combined with other data (typically on attitudes, beliefs, and behavior) for this purpose.

The most recent (1980) PUMS contain information on 32 population variables and 27 housing items. Population items added since 1970 include questions on commuting patterns, source of income, time spent looking for work, current language and ability to speak English, and ancestry. A significant change in 1980 was identifying a person in whose name a dwelling was owned or rented instead of a household head. Censuses from 1880 to 1970 used the term household head, with the implication that this person was male. The 1980 survey also introduced a more detailed classification of race.

Three PUMS are available to researchers, each based on a specific geographical scheme. Sample A is a sample of U.S. population and housing that identifies each state and most counties with populations of 100,000 or more, as well as some cities and groups of places with 100,000 or more inhabitants. Sample B is organized primarily on the basis of Standard Metropolitan Statistical Areas (SMSAs) and allows for differentiation between metropolitan and nonmetropolitan areas. Sample C encompasses census regions, divisions, 27 states, and the District of Columbia. All urban areas with over 800,000 inhabitants as well as about half the urban areas with populations between 200,000 and 800,000 are separately designated. Four types of areas are identified: inside central city, urban fringe, other urban, and rural. Three 1-in-1000 samples have also been prepared, one each from Samples A, B, and C (ICPSR, 1984).

Several aids for using the PUMS are available from the Bureau of the Census and other organizations. The technical documentation that accompanies the microdata files provides a description of the files, a discussion of census sampling procedures, a "data dictionary," and a glossary. The *Questionnaire Reference Book* (U.S. Department of Commerce, 1980) documents how the 1980 PUMS were gathered, and a textbook entitled *Census 80: Continuing the Fact-Finder Tradition* (Kaplan et al., 1980) provides an academic perspective on the 1980 census. Resources and data files are easily obtained by researchers. Data User Services at the Bureau of the Census and State Data Centers have PUMS for dissemination, as do the ICPSR and several other social data archives.

The Current Population Survey

The Current Population Survey (CPS) is a national study of the civilian noninstitutionalized population conducted monthly by the Bureau of the Census for the Bureau of Labor Statistics. Approximately 61,000 households are interviewed each month using a 4-8-4 rotational pattern. That is, households are interviewed for four consecutive months, then not interviewed for the next eight months, then interviewed for another four-month period. The CPS primarily monitors labor force activity and is the sole monthly source of estimates of total employment and unemployment. Information is collected on the characteristics of labor force participants, including data on workers' current occupations and industries. Since January 1980, the survey has also elicited data on "usual" number of hours worked per week and "usual" earnings. Most important, the CPS provides demographic and economic time series data on the U.S. population.

Beyond the information collected every month, regular and special (i.e., one-time) supplements enhance the survey's utility for social research. Each year, the March CPS collects extensive background data on every member of each sample household. Among the variables contained in these Annual Demographic Files are household structure and family relationships, personal employment history, education, and basic demographic characteristics (age, race, sex, and so on). The May supplements have frequently emphasized multiple job-holding and adult education. The October supplements have stressed educational topics, particularly school enrollment, while the November supplements have concentrated on voting in general elections. Other recurring supplements have focused on marital history, fertility, birth expectations, and immunization against disease.

Documentation of the Current Population Survey has recently improved. Supplemental data are now processed at the same time as CPS core data. Supplements from 1978 on are immediately available, as are earlier supplements if they have been processed for previous users. Basic CPS data may typically be obtained from the Data User Services Division of the Census Bureau about two months after data collection. Annual Demographic Files (i.e., the March supplements) require approximately nine months to process. Finally, CPS data files may be acquired from the Data User Services Division of the Bureau of the Census, the Data and Program Library Service in Wisconsin, or the ICPSR.

American National Election Study

The ongoing American National Election Study series (see, e.g., Miller and Miller, 1976)[4] currently consists of more than 20 national surveys conducted by the Center for Political Studies and the Survey Research Center of the Institute for Social Research (CPS/SRC) at the University of Michigan. Originally designed and analyzed mainly by senior members of the CPS/SRC Political Behavior Program, the surveys are now supervised by a nine-member Board of Overseers, all social scientists (House, 1979). The National Election Study was established in 1948 to test a theory which proposed that voting decisions are explained by both long-term forces, such as party identification, and short-term influences, such as perceptions of candidates and issue positions. This "Michigan model," established in *The American Voter* (Campbell et al., 1960), has become the dominant paradigm for the study of electoral behavior in political science and has shaped subsequent surveys in the series (House, 1979; Rusk, 1982).

Personal interviews were conducted after the 1948 presidential election, before and after the presidential elections from 1952 to 1984, and after the congressional elections of 1958, 1962, 1966, 1970, 1974, 1978, and 1982. In addition, pilot studies to test new items were conducted in 1979 and 1983. Four panel studies are embedded in the series: a subset of respondents from the 1956 study was reinterviewed in 1958 and 1960; a second panel of respondents was contacted in 1972, 1974, and 1976; a year-long panel consisting of four data collections was built into the 1980 survey (ICPSR, 1984); and a subset of respondents from the 1982 national election study was reinterviewed by telephone for the 1983 pilot study. Except for the smaller 1948, 1979, and 1983 studies, each survey consists of interviews with 1000 to 2700 respondents. A multistage sample selection procedure results in a representative national sample of adults residing in private households within the 48 contiguous United States.

Each national election study contains between 50 and 2000 variables. A set of core questions replicated across the surveys asks about evaluations of the major parties and candidates, party identification, issue positions, and voting behavior. Also regularly included are: (1) attitudes toward various social groups; (2) assessments of the major foreign and domestic problems facing the country; (3) an evaluation of personal financial well-being; (4) exposure to the mass media; (5) social psychological orientations (e.g., trust in people and in government); and (6) demographic and socioeconomic characteristics such as age, sex, race, education, occupation, income, religious affiliation, and family composition. More recently, two new categories have been incorporated: contextual variables (i.e., aggregate data on respondents' census tracts and election data on congressional districts) and items exploring the influence of social networks on voting decisions. The 37-year span of the series and the comparability of many of the core variables make these surveys especially appropriate for trend studies.

The national election studies may be employed to investigate a wide variety of nonpolitical as well as political topics. For example, studies have tested alienation, relative deprivation, and social conflict theories of participation in conventional political activism (Sayles, 1983) and examined the determinants of class consciousness (Vanneman and Pampel, 1977). At present, a good deal of political science research using the studies looks at contextual effects on electoral behavior and the dynamics of voting behavior in congressional and senatorial elections. In addition, the development of statistical techniques for analyzing panel data has stimulated the investigation of endogenous influences on voting. The ANES data file and a bibliography of studies that have employed these surveys may be obtained from the ICPSR.

National Longitudinal Surveys of Labor Market Experience

The National Longitudinal Surveys (Parnes, 1980) are a joint project of the Office of Manpower Policy, Evaluation, and Research of the U.S. Department of Labor, the Center for Human Resource Research at Ohio State University, and the Bureau of the Census. Begun under

Herbert Parnes and continuing under Michael Borus, their purpose has been to provide panel data on the labor market experience of four groups of interest to policymakers. At the study's inception, the respondents sampled were young men and women aged 14 to 24, women 30 to 44 years old, and men 49 to 59 years old.

All of the men were first interviewed in person in 1966, the older women in 1967, and the young women in 1968. Each group was surveyed annually, usually in person, for the first several years, and then at least biennially either in person or by telephone for a total of 15 years. The men and women were surveyed 11 times, the young men and young women a dozen times. Each of the four groups was a national probability sample of approximately 5000 individuals, including an oversample of blacks in order to ensure adequate numbers.

In a new panel study begun in 1979, national probability samples of young men and women aged 14 to 21 are being interviewed annually in order to replicate the earlier study of youth cohorts. The new youth samples contain approximately 5700 young women and 5700 young men, plus 1300 members of the Armed Forces selected under funding from the Department of Defense. Blacks, Hispanics, and economically disadvantaged whites in this cohort are oversampled.

The National Longitudinal Surveys contain measures of labor market experience (e.g., labor force status and current and past job characteristics), socioeconomic variables (e.g., migration, education and training, health, marital and family characteristics, financial characteristics, military service, and job and work attitudes) and some contextual variables (e.g., local area unemployment rates). These surveys may be used for studies of labor supply, child care, intergenerational mobility, marital instability, sex discrimination, and labor demand. They also permit investigation of human capital and status attainment models, unemployment, the job search, social psychological influences on labor market experience, aging and men's labor force participation and retirement, and methodological issues (reviewed in Bielby et al., 1979; Daymont and Andrisani, 1983), as well as research on women's roles (Mott et al., 1983). One review indicates that the panel design could be more fully exploited, for example, to test life-cycle and developmental theories of labor market behavior, or to investigate the effects of aging and changes in health on labor market experience (Bielby et al., 1979).

The *National Longitudinal Surveys Handbook, 1982* also provides a bibliography of research using the data and is available free of charge from the Center of Human Resource Research, the Ohio State University, 5701 N. High Street, Worthington, OH 43085. Data from the National Longitudinal Surveys are also available from the center. The charge for each cohort's cumulated data file and documentation is $300. The NLS data files are also held by the ICPSR.

Panel Study of Income Dynamics

The Panel Study of Income Dynamics (PSID; Duncan, 1980), now sponsored by the National Science Foundation, was initiated by the Office of Economic Opportunity. Conducted annually since 1968 by the Institute for Social Research at the University of Michigan, its purpose is to investigate the determinants of family income dynamics, with special emphasis on variables that can be influenced by public policy. The principal investigators are Greg J. Duncan and James N. Morgan.

The original sample consisted of low-income families augmented with a representative cross-section of the U.S. civilian household population. Since then, all new families formed by members of panel families have been added to the sample. Interviews are conducted with household heads, either male or female. Interviews with wives of male household heads were also conducted in 1976 and 1985.

To date, there are 15 volumes of documentation for the study. The cumulated surveys contain well over 7000 variables, including many items that are repeated across surveys. Two types of files are available, one employing the family and the other using the individual as the unit of analysis. The individual file incorporates records for each respondent, plus information about his or her family for each interview year. The family file provides data about household members as a unit. Elder (1985) provides a guide to using the files.

The theoretical model underlying the PSID posits that changes in economic status are explained by demographic and socioeconomic background variables, environmental conditions, attitudes, and economic behavior. Background variables include age, sex, race, education, and family composition. Environmental variables, such as county unemployment rate, level of public school expenditures, and degree of urbanization of respondent's residence, indicate access to resources.

Attitudes include indexes of aspiration-ambition, trust-hostility, and personal efficacy. Measures of economic behavior relate to planning ahead, risk avoidance, and connectedness to sources of help and information. Some attitude measures that were originally included have been eliminated because of their poor predictive power.

To date, the Institute for Social Research has published ten volumes of findings from the PSID in a series entitled *Five Thousand American Families-Patterns of Economic Progress* (Morgan et al., 1974-1983). This series reports analyses conducted by the PSID research staff and provides abstracts of secondary analysis in progress. In addition to testing models of family income dynamics, the PSID has been used to study the life course, residential mobility, labor supply, fertility, disability, time use, family composition, reliance on public assistance, consumption, transportation, and methodological issues. PSID data files may be acquired through the ICPSR, where a bibliography of research using the PSID is maintained.

Surveys of Consumers

The Surveys of Consumers (formerly the Surveys of Consumer Attitudes and Behavior; Economic Behavior Program, 1976) are conducted under the direction of Richard T. Curtin at the Survey Research Center of the University of Michigan. Begun over 35 years ago, they were conducted three times a year during the 1950s and quarterly from 1960 to 1977. Since 1978 they have been conducted monthly (Curtin, 1982). The surveys were designed to test George Katona's theory of behavioral economics. This theory proposes that changes in consumer attitudes and expectations, such as optimism or pessimism about the economy, are leading indicators of aggregate economic activity inasmuch as they influence consumers' decisions regarding discretionary expenditures (Katona, 1975).

Each survey contains 40 core questions in five topic areas: (1) expectations and assessments of changes in personal finances, both long- and short-term, as well as changes in family real income during the previous year; (2) perceptions of present business conditions and expected changes in unemployment rates, prices, and interest rates, as well as confidence in government economic policy; (3) consumers' appraisals of market conditions, such as whether it is a good time to buy a house, car, or household durable, and their vehicle purchase intentions; (4) indicators of consumer behavior such as the ownership and purchase of financial instruments (investments), cars, houses, and consumer durables, as well as the incurrence and amount of debt; and (5) demographic characteristics, such as age, education, occupation, income, household size and composition, and geographic location. In addition to these five topics, each survey elicits opinions about economic developments during that period, such as a recession.

Approximately 1200 to 1600 dwelling units are sampled. The samples are representative of private households in the contiguous United States and are stratified by geographic region and metropolitan area size. A rotating panel design is used in which each respondent is interviewed twice. In a given survey, approximately half the respondents are new and half were previously interviewed six months earlier. This rotating panel design lends itself to four research designs: single cross-sectional studies, time-series analysis using successive cross-sectional surveys, single-panel studies, and time-series analysis of pooled panel surveys (Curtin, 1982). The Surveys of Consumers are available from the ICPSR.

Health Data

Coincident with growth in the health care industry, our nation's health statistical systems have expanded, and data pertaining to health status, health care services, and health-related expenditures are increasingly available. Despite this expansion, however, the supply of available data has lagged behind the demand, and problems persist. Variability between data sets is the major problem, involving non-uniformity in the reporting of data and a lack of common definitions for terms that appear across surveys.

Many health databases are available for secondary analysis, and the November 1983 issue of *Review of Public Data Use* provides a comprehensive inventory of publicly available, machine-readable health-related data files (Mullner et al., 1983). This listing briefly describes surveys conducted by both public and private sector organizations and provides information on the sponsor, purpose, scope, sampling procedures, frequency, availability, and content of each study. Databases included are usually representative national samples, and all include current data (collected after 1975).

The topics covered by health surveys generally fall into three categories. One category emphasizes individual health, including health attitudes, self-reports of health and illness, and objective health indicators such as physical examinations and laboratory test results. A second grouping focuses on health resources and health services utilization, encompassing studies of health facilities, health providers, and patterns of use by patients. A third substantive emphasis is health care economics, with surveys ranging from those monitoring the growth of the medical care industry to those examining emerging payment patterns.

The primary resource for statistics on health and related topics (e.g., vital events) is the National Center for Health Statistics (NCHS). *A Catalog of Public Use Data Tapes from the National Center for Health Statistics* is released annually and is available, free of charge, upon request. Machine-readable data files and accompanying documentation from NCHS surveys are sold through the National Technical Information Service (see Appendix A).

Until the late 1950s, health data in this country were sparse. Since 1957, however, the NCHS has conducted a number of continuing and specialized surveys. Two of the most important current general population surveys, the National Health Interview Survey (NHIS) and the National Health and Nutrition Examination Survey (NHANES), are described below.

National Health Interview Survey

A continuing survey implemented in 1957, intended to examine the effects of illness and poor health on disability and physical limitation, later became the National Health Interview Survey. Through weekly household interviews, the NHIS collects data on a range of health-related topics. These include the incidence of acute illness and accidental injury, the prevalence of chronic illness and impairment, the extent of disability, and the utilization of health care services. The survey is based on a multistage national sample of the civilian noninstitutionalized population of the 50 states and Washington, D.C. Approximately 40,000 households are sampled each year, and information is obtained for roughly 110,000 people (although this number is decreasing with the decline in family size). All persons 17 years of age and older are interviewed, while health information on children is obtained from an adult, usually the mother.

A core set of repeated health, socioeconomic, and demographic items constitute the bulk of the questionnaire and facilitate trend analysis. The interview employs a body systems approach that identifies chronic diseases according to the system of the body (digestive, circulatory, and so on) involved. Until 1978, the NHIS collected data on conditions involving only one body system each year. Six separate representative subsamples are now chosen annually. Each subsample is queried about one system, allowing concurrent estimates of conditions associated with all six systems. Supplements to the core questionnaire emphasize current health topics such as smoking, immunization, and home health care. Since 1969 the data have been organized into five different record types: person, condition, household, hospital, and doctor visit. Basic person data are included in each of the files.

National Health and Nutrition Examination Survey

The National Health and Nutrition Examination Survey (NHANES) furnishes direct data about the health status of the U.S. population through physical and laboratory examinations. The NHANES, begun in 1971, expands on the 1969 National Health Examination Survey (NHES), which was designed to measure and monitor national health. The NHANES emphasizes nutrition as a health determinant. Data are collected on the prevalence of specific diseases, and survey results are used to establish normative health values for the population.

A multistage stratified probability sample of noninstitutionalized households is drawn, and respondents are selected on a probabilistic basis. Groups thought to be at high risk for malnutrition—for example, low-income families, preschool children, the elderly, and women of childbearing age—are oversampled. Sampling weights provided for variables such as age, sex, race, and so forth allow the sample to be adjusted to reflect the population of interest.

In the NHANES, medical examinations are conducted in mobile examination centers and include ophthalmological, dermatological, and dental exams; a series of hematological and biochemical tests; and a set of anthropometric measurements. Also included in the NHANES surveys are household and individual background interviews, a 24-hour dietary intake recall interview, a food frequency interview, and a food program questionnaire.

Data are available for two completed NHANES surveys, and for three waves of its forerunner, the NHES. The NHES surveys had particular age foci. Wave I (1959-1962) concentrated on adults aged 18 to 79, Wave II (1963-1965) studied children aged 6 to 11, and Wave III (1966-1970) examined youths aged 12 to 17. The NHANES I and II surveys each had a target sample size of approximately 30,000 and a response rate of over 73 percent. The upper age limit for both of these surveys was 74, while the lower limit was one year during NHANES I (1971-1975) and six months during NHANES II (1976-1980). NHANES I sampled only people in the coterminous United States, while NHANES II sampled people in all 50 states. The NHANES I data file includes a subsample of people aged 25 to 44 for whom there were detailed physical examination data on four target areas: respiratory, cardiovascular, arthritic, and aural. An epidemiological follow-up conducted on this subsample in the early 1980s will supply data on the slow-acting consequences of long-term and low dosage exposure to a variety of environmental and dietary factors in light of social and demographic characteristics. These data also permit estimates of the incidence of selected conditions.

The data contained in the NHIS and NHANES files are useful to program planners and evaluators, health educators, epidemiologists, and market researchers. They have been used in illness prevention and in planning and improving health delivery services. Direct measurement data collected in the NHANES have been used by industrial groups and in medical texts and references. Health data also have potential beyond purely applied uses. For example, they can be used to construct models to explain use patterns or to test theories of increased illness, disability, or good health among particular groups. The National Technical Information Service supplies the NHIS and NHANES data and accompanying documentation at a cost of between $125 and $305 per NHANES tape and $45 per NHIS tape.

Referencing Data

As the above descriptions of archives and data sets indicate, the availability and use of machine-readable data files have increased rapidly. Bibliographic control of these files, however, is minimal. There is currently no union list of files, nor is it generally possible to access information by variable. In the next several years, systems will probably be developed that will increase the ease with which researchers can locate data. Since secondary analysis of survey data is a relatively recent phenomenon, an official standard for referencing data sets has yet to be established. Data archivists and seasoned secondary analysts agree, however, that machine-readable data files need to be referenced in much the same way that books are cited, so that others may easily consult the original source. Referencing should minimally include the principal investigator and date of the study, the name of the data set, the fact that it is a machine-readable data file, the producer of the tape, and the archive from which the data file was obtained.

3. MAKING EFFECTIVE USE
OF EXISTING SURVEY DATA

The available data files discussed in Chapter 2 give an indication of the many topics that can be examined through secondary research. Secondary analysis is extremely versatile in that it can be applied to studies designed to understand the present or the past, to understand change, to examine phenomena comparatively, or to replicate and/or extend previous studies (Hyman, 1972: 11-24). This chapter begins by reviewing several research designs for the secondary analysis of survey data.

In designing secondary analyses, analyzing the results, and drawing conclusions, researchers face a number of potential problems. Some are a part of all survey analysis, while others are unique to studies employing existing data. The remainder of the chapter is devoted to discussing methodological problems of secondary analysis and possible solutions to these problems.

Research Designs

CROSS-SECTIONAL DESIGNS

Cross-sectional studies, which examine a phenomenon at one time, can be used in addressing the entire range of research questions that surveys have been designed to investigate. These questions include "fundamental social phenomena" such as ideology, social mobility, and political behavior as well as comparisons of social groups (Hyman, 1972). Cross-sectional designs may employ a single survey or multiple surveys. When multiple surveys containing equivalent indicators are used in a study, the surveys may either be treated separately as internal replications or pooled. Later in this chapter we discuss how to determine significance when multiple surveys are treated as internal replications, as well as statistical issues to consider when pooling surveys to study small populations.

DESIGNS FOR TEMPORAL ANALYSIS

We discuss five types of research designs for temporal analysis: trend, cohort, panel, event history, and time series. Trend studies make comparisons of cross-sectional data for two or more points in time and so require roughly comparable items and samples. Their purpose is to investigate change in the level or distribution of a variable, or in the relationships among variables for entire populations or subpopulations (Glenn and Frisbie, 1977). Trends may be differentiated or disaggregated (Hyman, 1972).

Differentiating a trend means plotting it separately for various dimensions or aspects of the dependent variable and hence requires multiple measures. Differentiating a trend can provide useful information on the specificity or generality of changes (Hyman, 1972). For example, trends in attitudes toward racial integration have been measured by the five-item Treiman scale, which appears in the General Social Survey. When the items are plotted separately, it can be seen that change does not proceed uniformly across all dimensions. For example, attitudes toward interracial marriages have changed more rapidly in a pro-integration direction than have attitudes toward residential integration (Taylor et al., 1978).

Disaggregating trends—that is, plotting them separately for subgroups such as those defined by age or education—enables the researcher to discover the structural locations in society in which change is occurring (Hyman, 1972). Subgroups used in disaggregating a trend are chosen according to theoretical or practical grounds. For example, disaggregating by region is important in explaining changes in racial attitudes because the North and South may change at different rates. Trends that occur uniformly in a population, on the other hand, are not located in any one place in society but rather reflect national or macro-social phenomena, and disaggregating merely confirms this (Hyman, 1972).

When trends are disaggregated, a number of hypotheses about patterns of change may be tested (Taylor, 1976). These are: (1) no group differences exist and no change has occurred; (2) existing group differences have remained constant; (3) group differences are either increasing or decreasing in a steady linear fashion; or (4) levels or distributions of variables and also patterns of relationships among variables have changed suddenly and erratically as a result of various social forces. Taylor (1976) shows how to test these hypotheses with trend data, and Hyman (1972) reviews underlying theoretical explanations for various patterns of change.

Cohort studies investigate characteristics of cohorts at two or more points in time (Glenn and Frisbie, 1977). The term "cohort" refers to any group that has experienced some major life event (such as entry into the labor force) during a designated interval, but it usually refers to birth cohorts. Cohort analysis designs are especially well suited for studying aging and also social, political, and cultural change. For example, Glenn (1980) has used cohort analysis to test the hypothesis that susceptibility to attitude change declines with age. Glenn (1977) reviews sources of data appropriate for cohort analysis, citing especially national survey data series available from the ICPSR and the Roper Center.

The decision about which cohorts are particularly meaningful to study is one place where a grounding in theory and substantive knowledge of historical events is particularly important. Researchers often study cohorts on whose individual biographies historical events may have left an especially deep imprint—for example, Elder's (1974) study of a cohort that experienced the Great Depression.

The typical strategy for a cohort analysis is to construct a "standard cohort table" (Glenn, 1977) whose rows are groups representing the life event of interest (typically age groups) and whose columns are survey years. Ideally, the interval between surveys should equal the width of each age group. When that is the case, one can make cross-sectional intercohort comparisons by reading down each column, examine trends for each age group by reading across the rows, and follow intracohort trends by reading diagonally down and to the right. Glenn (1977) explains how to construct cohort tables when construction of a standard cohort table is impossible.

The object of a cohort analysis is to separate the observed variation in a cohort table into effects due to aging, cohort effects resulting from distinctive historical location and experiences, and period effects caused by events unique to each era. The problem is that two of these effects are always confounded with each other. For example, when reading across the rows, cohort and period effects may both account for observed variation. Since these effects cannot be unconfounded statistically, it is possible to make an interpretation of their relative contribution only by importing evidence from outside the data; hence any cohort analysis must be theoretically informed.

Panel studies utilize data collected at more than one time for the same persons or entities. Only panel designs permit the study of changes among respondents rather than simply among populations or subpopulations. As a consequence, panel analysis is one of the best means for studying such topics as individual change over the life course or processes of individual mobility and attainment. For example, the PSID (discussed in Chapter 2) has been used in a set of studies that apply a life-course perspective to human development (Elder, 1985). The number of available panel data files is increasing. For example, panel components are now being built into the National Election Studies for the purpose of examining the dynamics of political attitudes and behavior (for a discussion of statistical techniques for panel analysis, see Kessler and Greenberg, 1981).

Event-history designs, an extension of panel analysis, are used for studying the determinants of persons' or other units' rates of change between different states of a categorical variable for a given period of time, using a continuous-time Markov model. This design requires panel data on the sequence of categories of the dependent variable that a unit occupies during a given period of time, and also on the timing of all moves in each sequence (Tuma et al., 1979). Types of data that event-history designs could fruitfully exploit include surveys such as the PSID, which record both the timing and sequence of life-course events. For instance, an event-history design was used to study the effects of varying levels of financial support from the Denver and Seattle Income-Maintenance Experiments on rates of female marital dissolution (Tuma et al., 1979). See also Allison (1984) and Tuma and Hannan (1984) for detailed treatments of the statistical techniques used in event-history analysis.

Time-series designs are used to describe changing patterns of phenomena, to explain the sources of those changes, and to make predictions about future changes. Political scientists, for example, have analyzed changes in presidential popularity and their relationship to economic fluctuations and events such as wars. Time-series designs require observations on quantitative variables at many points in time for the same unit of analysis, such as consumer confidence scores for the United States measured at monthly intervals. Time-series models may be either nonlagged or lagged. In a nonlagged model both the endogenous and exogenous variables are observed at the same point in time, while in the lagged case past values of endogenous and/or exogenous variables are used to predict the endogenous variable (Ostrom, 1978: 10). Time-series analysis uses a regression framework but faces particular statistical problems because error terms of successive observations are likely to be correlated. Ostrom (1978) provides a detailed introduction to the statistical techniques used in time-series designs.

CROSS-NATIONAL STUDIES

The wide availability of cross-national survey data from other countries (see Chapter 2) suggests enormous potential for cross-national studies. Indeed, cross-national or comparative studies are a paramount goal of the social sciences. They enable us to know whether observed social phenomena and relationships are universal or confined to a particular nation or type of society. Cross-national designs, like cross-sectional studies, lend themselves to comparisons of social groups (e.g., social classes) and to the examination of fundamental phenomena (Hyman, 1972). Roos (1985), for example, has analyzed the relationship between sex and earnings in nine industrialized countries. Cross-national comparisons may also be made of changes over time—that is, they may be extensions of national panel, cohort, trend, and time-series studies. In one study, Nieme and Westholm (1983) used panel data to compare attitude stability in Sweden and the United States.

Hyman (1972) recommends that cross-national studies be undertaken only by experienced secondary analysts. Such studies are rife with potential problems of both item and sample comparability, problems that will be addressed later in this chapter. Moreover, conducting cross-national studies requires a great deal of knowledge about the cultural and social contexts and the histories of the nations involved. Even seemingly similar countries may be dissimilar along some important dimensions. The problem is compounded when using comparative surveys conducted at different times, because it is difficult to determine whether differences are due to enduring cultural and social features or to transient factors. Even simultaneous surveys control only for events impinging on both countries, not for unique events within the countries. Hyman (1972) advocates the "principle of similarity" as a research strategy: Choose countries whose many similar features serve as controls, but whose differences represent cultural or social structural variation. For example, Roos (1985) limited her comparison to industrialized countries in which the pattern of women's labor force participation was similar.

CONTEXTUAL DESIGNS

The growing realization in the social sciences that a variety of phenomena must be understood within the context in which they occur has renewed interest in investigating contextual effects. Contextual designs merge survey data on individuals with data on the characteristics of their environments (macro-level variables) in order to explain individual-level variables. In the simplest models, the behavior of the ith individual in the jth group is explained by a combination of individual-level independent variables and by the group mean of either the independent or the dependent variable (Blalock, 1984: 353). These effects may be additive or interactive, and there may be multiple relevant contexts.

Contextual variables may be global variables—that is, macro-level variables that do not simply summarize micro-level variables—or they may be aggregated from individual-level variables. For example, whether a child's school is private or public is a global variable, while classroom size is aggregated from individual-level data.

Although contextual designs in secondary analysis are not new, only recently have the statistical issues involved in making inferences from contextual data been clarified. Stipak and Hensler (1982) discuss some possible solutions to the problems of specification error, measurement error, and multicollinearity. Blalock (1984) provides a review of theoretical and methodological issues that must be considered when formulating and testing contextual effects models. These include the question of self-selection into contexts, the difficulty of specifying the temporal sequences and mechanisms in and through which contextual effects operate, and the complications that arise when multiple relevant contexts are nested or overlapping.

Variable Operationalization

As mentioned in Chapter 1, the major limitation of secondary analysis is that surveys may not contain precise indicators of the concepts the secondary analyst wants to study. When this happens, the researcher must attempt to develop creative schemes for measuring items of interest. It is often the case that several items can be combined in various ways to represent the concepts that the researcher has in mind.

Although examples of creative variable operationalization (i.e., finding measures for given concepts) can be found throughout the literature on virtually all topics, recent studies in stratification that operationalize quasi-Marxian social class categories serve as examples of how researchers have productively drawn on existing survey data. In each case, discrete social classes were defined and employed in a class analysis. This type of analysis, accounting for an emerging body of research in the field of social stratification, uses a Marxist theoretical framework for understanding empirical events. The class perspective looks at how social relations originating in the existing mode of production give rise to conflict and to the possibility of structural change.

Wright and Perrone (1977) employed secondary data from the 1969 "Survey of Working Conditions" (Quinn et al., 1970) and the 1972-1973 "Quality of Employment Survey" (Quinn et al., 1973) in order to compare the power of class with that of occupational status in explaining income differences. The authors' conceptualization of social class modifies the traditional Marxist analysis of class structure in capitalist society that utilizes ownership of the means of production, purchase of the labor power of others, and sale of one's own labor power as criteria for class differentiation, and that distinguishes capitalists, workers, and the petty bourgeoisie. Recognizing the need for a scheme that more accurately reflects contemporary capitalism, Wright and Perrone extended this basic model to take into account an authority structure to some extent separated from ownership.

Neither of the data files employed by Wright and Perrone (1977) included straightforward measures of social class membership, thus defined. Based on three questions included in the 1969 surveys, however, the authors were able to construct a class typology similar to the expanded Marxian scheme they had conceptualized. The questions were: (1) "Most of the time on this job, do you work for yourself or someone else?" (2) "If you are self-employed, are there any people who work for you and are paid by you?" and (3) "Do you supervise anybody as part of your job?". Based on possible combinations of answers to these questions, five social class categories were identified (see Table 2). Wright and Perrone found that while both their social class typology and status (as measured by Duncan SEI scores) contributed to income, class explained a greater proportion of the variance.[5]

Sometimes operationalization requires incorporating information from outside a survey. Using the 1970 U.S. Census Public Use Sample, Engelberg (1981) has defined discrete social classes in order to evaluate

54

TABLE 2
Wright and Perrone's Class Typology

	Self-Employed	Have Employees	Have Subordinate on the Job	Employed
Employers	yes	yes	yes	no
Managers	no	no	yes	yes
Workers	no	no	no	yes
Petty bourgeoisie	yes	no	no	no
Ambiguous	yes	no	yes	no

SOURCE: Wright and Perrone (1977: 34).

the sex and class components of structural inequality. The dimensions used for assigning individuals to social strata were: ownership of the means of production, authority over others in the workplace, and skill exercised on the job.

In the Census Public Use Sample data, only one of the three criteria for class membership, ownership of the means of production, was measured. Ownership was determined by responses to the variable "class of worker," which identified those who were self-employed. Skill and authority were based on the *Dictionary of Occupational Titles* (U.S. Department of Labor, 1965), which gives six-digit codes describing occupations. Skill was measured by an occupation's relation to data and things, while authority was considered a function of each occupation's relation to people. By utilizing information outside the actual data file, Engelberg was able to develop a social class typology with four basic categories (see Table 3). In this scheme, the entrepreneurial bourgeoisie corresponds to the traditional petty bourgeoisie, and the managerial bourgeoisie is like the new petty bourgeoisie discussed by Poulantzas (1975). The Marxist proletariat is divided into two working class groups on the basis of skill.

Once social strata were identified, each stratum was separated into male and female groups. Utilizing discriminant function analysis, Engelberg was able to determine that sex and class do not operate independently of one another in the social system. Specifically, sex appears to influence social class of destination and then to mediate the impact of class membership on social and economic rewards.

Evaluating Existing Indicators

With many surveys, variable operationalization is not a problem because multiple measures are available. Moreover, items frequently

TABLE 3
Engelberg's Social Class Typology

	Skill	Authority	Ownership of the Means of Production
Entrepreneurial bourgeoisie	–	(high)	yes
Managerial bourgeoisie	high	high	no
Skilled working class	high	low	no
Unskilled working class	low	low	no

SOURCE: Engelberg (1981: 47).

constitute a data series because they have been repeated across surveys. Researchers often have simply summed the designated items to construct indexes, sometimes after performing an exploratory factor analysis to assess whether items did indeed constitute a single dimension. Recently, however, researchers have begun to use covariance structure analytic techniques such as those in the LISREL program to more critically evaluate the relationships among such existing measures (see Long, 1983a, 1983b). Covariance structure analytic techniques allow a researcher to test models of the relationships between items. The researcher predicts which items will comprise each factor or construct, whether the constructs that were posited will be correlated with each other, and further whether any of the error terms of the items will be correlated (an assumption that is not allowed by exploratory factor analytic techniques). A chi-square test of goodness of fit is used to evaluate how well the posited model reproduces the observed correlations or covariances among the items; the smaller the chi-square, the better the fit. The LISREL technique also provides information about which model parameters need to be respecified in order to improve the fit. That is, the information enables the researcher to make an improved prediction about which variables will make up each construct, whether the constructs will be correlated with each other, and so forth.

An illustration of this technique is provided by Acock et al.'s (1985) analysis of the six Michigan Survey Research Center items designed to measure political efficacy. Three of the items were conceived of as indicators of internal political efficacy, and three of external efficacy. The adequacy of both a one-factor (general political efficacy) and a two-factor (internal and external political efficacy) solution was tested using data from the 1976 National Election Study (Miller and Miller, 1976). An index constructed by simply summing all six items assumes that a unidimensional construct of efficacy accounts for all of the covariances among the six items, that all six items contribute equally to the construct, and that the indicators of efficacy are measured without error. Acock et al. (1985) tested a number of one-factor and two-factor models of the relationships between the items. The tests revealed that one of the internal efficacy items had an especially poor fit with the model and so was excluded from all further analyses. The most theoretically and empirically satisfactory model had two factors corresponding to internal and external efficacy. The two factors were highly correlated, the items did not contribute equally to the factors, and there were correlations between the error terms of some of the items. Knowing how the items that measure a concept are related to each other helps to guide analysis using the items.

As a further test of the model, the goodness of fit was evaluated separately for men and women, blacks and whites, other National Election Studies, and nations other than the United States. In those tests, successive constraints were imposed to test whether the efficacy items had the same structure across groups or surveys (i.e., whether the same variables loaded on each factor) and essentially the same factor loadings, and whether the between-factor correlations differed significantly across groups or surveys. In all but one instance, the goodness of fit remained satisfactory.

These analyses suggest that covariance structure analytic procedures such as those in the LISREL program may have great potential for researchers who wish to evaluate existing indicators of various concepts and employ them in analyses. First, these procedures identify items that are poor measures of a given concept so that these items may be excluded from analysis. Second, they show which items are most central to a concept by indicating the unequal contributions that items make to measuring given constructs. Third, by allowing constructs to be correlated, covariance analysis points to possible problems of multicollinearity that may arise when the correlated constructs are included as independent variables. Fourth, covariance structure analytic techniques correct for the substantial amount of measurement error that is found in many survey items.

Problems of Item Comparability

Trend and cross-cultural designs involve comparing equivalent items across surveys, thus raising potential problems of item comparability. One problem occurs when roughly comparable items have an unequal number of response categories, a situation often found with attitudinal surveys. In such cases, the researchers should not only make comparisons based on analysis of unrecoded responses but also summarize the results of the analysis when categories are collapsed to make the number of categories equal. For example, Niemi and Westholm (1983) compared the attitude stability of Swedish and U.S. respondents on several policy issues of varying degrees of abstractness. The U.S. surveys measured respondents' issue positions on a number of seven-point scales and dichotomies, while the Swedish surveys used four-, five-, and 11-point scales. After computing stability coefficients on the unrecoded scales, Niemi and Westholm made all five-, seven-, and 11-point scales into trichotomies and collapsed all the agree-disagree four-point scales into dichotomies. Collapsing the categories often yields results that differ somewhat from the original ones. In this case, the stability coefficients computed with the collapsed variables decreased as much as .06 (for the Swedish four-point agree-disagree items). In addition, the average differences between Sweden and the United States declined by .02.

Even variables with identical question "stems" and the same number of response categories may be noncomparable if the response alternatives of questions differ. For instance, suppose an item measuring subjective social class has the response categories "upper class," "upper middle class," "middle class," "working class," and "poor," while a similar item substitutes "lower class" for "poor." A larger proportion of people are likely to place themselves in the "working class" category, and a correspondingly smaller proportion in the bottom category, due to the greater stigma of being "lower class." Glenn (1977) and Smith (1981b) show how different response alternatives influence responses to similar questions that measure happiness.

Seemingly identical questions on different surveys may also be noncomparable when some are contingency questions—that is, questions that are asked as a result of the respondent's answer to the previous question. For example, suppose that on one survey respondents were asked to report their income only if they worked more than 20 hours per week, and on another survey all respondents were questioned about their income. The two questions could be made comparable (if possible) by identifying respondents from the second survey working less than 20 hours per week and excluding them from the analysis.

Sometimes filter questions are used to screen out respondents who do not have opinions on issues by presenting "Don't know" (DK), "No opinion," or "Haven't thought much about it" as acceptable responses.

By contrast, questions in standard form allow interviewers to accept DK responses only if respondents volunteer them (Schuman and Presser, 1981). Introducing a filter can increase the proportion of respondents in the DK category, though it does not usually alter the distribution of responses in the substantive categories. For purposes of charting trends or making cross-cultural comparisons, items can thus be made comparable by excluding the DK category from analysis.

Filtering has been found to have little effect on correlations of attitude items with background variables, but it sometimes significantly alters correlations between attitude items. A comparison of filtered and unfiltered attitude items using secondary data (Bishop et al., 1979) found that the presence of filters generally increased correlations between attitude items by excluding respondents without firm attitudes. The increase is likely to be negligible for items with a small number of DK's (Niemi and Westholm, 1983); however, when such "opinion floaters" are included, correlations among attitude items may increase. This opinion floater phenomenon seems to occur when respondents are asked about unfamiliar issues—for example, those requiring sophisticated knowledge of economic or foreign affairs. Respondents react by looking for cues or symbols in the item content which allow them to respond negatively or positively based on their beliefs about the goodness or badness of human nature. As a consequence, filtered and standard items should be compared very cautiously in studies investigating changes in relationships among attitude items (Martin, 1983; Schuman and Presser, 1981).

Researchers should also be cautious in equating items that present only one side of an issue with those offering two or more alternative views. Balanced and unbalanced versions of the same question sometimes yield different results, depending on the nature of the counterargument and respondent characteristics (Schuman and Presser, 1981). For example, in the preelection phase of the 1972 National Election Study series (Miller et al., 1972), 85 percent of the respondents agreed a great deal or somewhat that "many qualified women can't get good jobs; men with the same skills have much less trouble." In the postelection survey, respondents were given a balanced form of the question asking which of two statements they agreed with most, the one above or that "in general, men are more qualified than women for jobs that have more responsibility." In the second instance, 59 percent agreed with the first statement. Hence on some issues, presenting a counterargument can effectively introduce a new issue and lead to a nontrivial shift of opinion.

By contrast, comparing items that ask only if a respondent favors an issue with those that ask if the respondent favors or opposes the same issue is not likely to present problems of comparability. These two forms of unbalanced items have similar univariate distributions and correlations with respondent characteristics.

The context and sequence of survey items may also influence responses. That is, a question or set of questions may be placed differently with respect to other topics, or the sequence of individual items within a set of items may vary. The questions that precede an item suggest a frame of reference. They stimulate thinking about particular topics and encourage recall of experiences and knowledge that influence responses to later questions. There is speculation (but no definitive evidence), for example, that levels of confidence in institutions are slightly lower if the confidence questions follow a series of questions on alienation (Smith, 1981b). A context effect can also operate if respondents feel constrained to be consistent with their answers to earlier questions (Martin, 1983). For instance, respondents to the 1972 National Election Study who claimed to feel very warmly toward some group in society (e.g., blacks) may have felt that they also had to claim closeness to the group in order to be consistent with their earlier reply. These effects often operate even if unrelated items intervene between items that might influence each other (Schuman and Presser, 1981).

If a context effect is suspected, it is desirable to compare responses to equivalent items from additional surveys which do not appear to be contaminated by other items. Smith (1981b) suspected a context effect as a possible reason that NORC surveys often found significantly higher levels of personal happiness than did SRC surveys. A house effect, or a difference between survey organizations due to sampling procedures and interviewer training, was one possible explanation. He noted, however, that from 1973 to 1977, the NORC general happiness question immediately followed a marital happiness question on which responses were highly positive. Furthermore, the two items were strongly related (gamma = .75 for the pooled 1973-1977 surveys). To test for a context effect, Smith cross-tabulated general happiness by marital status (married versus not married)' and survey year (1973-1977 versus 1972, when there was no marital happiness question). The marital happiness question did appear to inflate general happiness. The difference between married and unmarried in the proportion "very happy" was greater in 1973-1977 (.209) than in 1972 (.163), a difference of the differences of .046. Although it was not statistically significant, Smith attempted to test whether this difference nevertheless represented a real context effect. He reduced the proportion of "very happy" married respondents in the 1973-1977 NORC surveys accordingly. To do this, he multiplied the proportion married in the pooled 1973-1977 surveys (.678) by the effect (−.046) and subtracted the result from the proportion "very happy" in 1973-1977. This decreased the proportion of "very happy" married respondents by .032, an adjustment that would reduce or eliminate most of the difference between the NORC and SRC surveys.

The meanings that respondents assign to questions tend to vary over time and by age as particular words or phrases gain or lose symbolic significance, thus raising the issue of temporal invalidity. For example, the meanings of the terms "liberal" and "conservative" have changed a great deal since the 1930s when questions measuring the dimension were first asked. At that time, an isolationist or noninterventionist stance on foreign affairs was indicative of a conservative position, while today the reverse is true. As a result, findings from cohort or trend studies using such items would have to be interpreted carefully, as would analyses employing items containing time-bound references such as "the president" (Glenn, 1977).

Demographic or structural change in the object of an attitude can also alter the meaning of a question. Changes in immigration patterns and in the occupational and geographic distribution of a social group may be accompanied by changing beliefs about and relations with the group (Hyman, 1972: 249). For example, a question measuring willingness to vote for a woman for president may take on a different meaning as more women run for and hold political office. Such developments need to be noted in interpreting shifts in intergroup relations. A cohort analyst, for example, would explain such change in terms of period rather than age effects.

Respondents can test for temporal validity when identically worded set of questions measuring some concept are available in surveys conducted at different points in time. Temporal validity may be evaluated by using covariance structure analytic techniques such as those in the LISREL program (see Long, 1983a, 1983b). These techniques assume that each concept (termed a latent construct or factor) is measured by multiple indicators that are assumed to be linear functions of this unmeasured construct plus some unknown unique variance, some of which is assumed to be measurement error. It is possible to estimate how well given indicators represent a latent construct by finding the epistemic correlations—that is, the degree of association between each indicator and the construct. Empirically, if the epistemic correlation between a given indicator and the latent construct that it is indirectly measuring are different at different times, the phenomenon being measured at the different times may not be the same. Whether or not the difference in the size of the epistemic correlations is due to chance alone can be tested by comparing the goodness of fit in a model in which the two parameters are constrained to be equal with a "free" model in which they are allowed to differ. If the goodness of fit is significantly better in the free model, then the measure is very likely not temporally valid.

Acock et al. (1985) performed a test of temporal validity in their assessment of the items used in the National Election Studies to measure political efficacy. As described earlier, the researchers developed and tested a model of the relationships between the political efficacy items on the 1976 National Election Study. As a test of whether the items were temporally valid, the researchers specified that the same model held in the 1972 and 1980 surveys as in 1976. That is, the items were predicted to result in the same factors and to have essentially the same correlations with the constructs in all years. Further, between-factor correlations were predicted to remain the same. Even with these constraints applied, the goodness of fit with the 1976 model was satisfactory for both the 1972 and the 1980 data. Hence the measure of political efficacy can be said to be temporally valid for that period of time.

An analogue to temporal invalidity may occur in cross-cultural studies (Martin, 1983). Questions may have very different meanings depending on the cultural context. For example, cultural variation in how physical symptoms are interpreted and treated could lead to differential reporting of illness or disability on a health survey and to incorrect conclusions unless a researcher brings knowledge of such cultural differences to his or her interpretation of the findings. Covariance structure analytic techniques can also be applied to cross-national data to test whether the relationships between items and the concepts they are measuring differ across cultures.

Items that are characterized by short-term or cyclical variation present special problems to the secondary analyst. Those that fluctuate seasonally, such as leisure activities, have larger error variances. As a result, a greater difference between surveys is needed for significance. In such instances, researchers studying trends should use at least three or four surveys spread over all seasons for each time period and make comparisons between surveys conducted at approximately the same time of year (Glenn, 1977). Seasonal fluctuations may also differ nationally. Some attitudes or behaviors vary over the long term with regularly occurring events, such as elections, or with less predictable events, such as the business cycle. An apparent trend may simply be an artifact of data having been collected at different points in a cycle (Glenn, 1977).

Problems of Sample Comparability

Problems of sample comparability are of potential concern in secondary research designs in which surveys are to be compared. Both trend and cross-national comparisons are vulnerable to differences in sample design. Changes over time in methods of locating and selecting respondents have resulted in changes in sample composition. Both the Survey Research Center at the University of Michigan and the National Opinion Research Center use full probability designs in which respondents from specified households are selected at random (see the discussion in this chapter on the problem of sampling error). However, until the mid-1950s, the NORC used quota samples in which interviewers had discretion over respondent selection as long as they met their quotas. For the General Social Survey, the NORC formerly used a modified probability sample (a quota sample at the block level), introduced full probability sampling for half of the sample in 1975, and only since 1977 has used full probability sampling.

Commercial polling organizations also differ in their sample selection procedures and may have particular sample biases. Harris polls require interviewers to meet a 50-50 sex quota (Martin, 1983). The interviewer decides whether to interview a male or a female adult in a given household, then randomly selects a respondent from a list of all household adults of that sex. Gallup polls are the most problematic. Until the 1950s they utilized quota sampling in which interviewers had complete discretion over respondent selection, as long as they filled their quotas. In addition, the early Gallup surveys were designed to be representative of the voting population and hence underrepresented women, blacks, southerners, and persons with little education. These quota samples thus underrepresented low-status segments of the population and overrepresented persons who are friendly and readily available.

Gradually, changes have been introduced that have made samples representative of the noninstitutionalized civilian adult population

(Glenn, 1975, provides a chart of the changes). The result is that there has been an artifactual decrease in level of education in the Gallup surveys over time resulting from the progressive inclusion of groups with lower education. Furthermore, variables that are highly correlated with sex, race, region, and education are apt to be biased. One solution is to standardize estimates in order to correct for the underrepresentation of groups and to see whether the corrected data yield different results; Glenn (1977) provides examples of how to adjust data for the underrepresentation of either one or two groups. Another solution is to limit comparisons by conducting separate analyses for subsets of surveys that use the same sampling method. Researchers can also introduce the biased variable as a control in analyzing change. Martin (1983) reviews sampling biases typical of various research organizations.

In addition to changes in methods of locating and selecting respondents, the increasing use of telephone rather than face-to-face interviews raises issues of sample noncomparability due to differences in population coverage and nonresponse. By omitting households without telephones, national telephone surveys tend to underrepresent low-income households; those with nonwhite heads; those with single, divorced, or separated heads; those headed by persons under 35; those in rental dwellings; those in the South; and those in rural nonfarm areas. Although the percentage of households without telephones has declined over time, weighting or standardization may still be needed in order to make these samples representative.

Besides noncoverage (i.e., failure to include some elements of the population in the sampling frame), other problems of sample noncomparability occur when the distribution of a survey variable does not equal the population distribution due to unequal probability of selection, sampling fluctuation, or nonresponse (i.e., differential response rates within subclasses of the sample). Most surveys include sampling weights as a variable that is used to adjust for unequal probabilities of selection. Using the weights may sometimes inflate the number of cases, as in the 1976 National Election Study (Miller and Miller, 1976), in which some respondents were assigned a weight of 1.0 and others a weight of 1.5. In these instances, it is possible both to weight the sample and to return it to its original size, which is accomplished by weighting the sample by a new weight variable achieved by dividing the original weight by its mean.

When the sample distribution of some important variable of interest does not equal the population distribution due to nonresponse and sampling fluctuation, the sample may be weighted in accordance with the known population distribution. For example, in a 12-nation comparison of women's and men's status attainment, Roos (1985) required sample surveys that accurately estimated the proportion of the labor force that was male and female in each country. Many of the estimates in the sample surveys did not equal population proportions, presumably as a consequence of differential nonresponse rates. Roos therefore obtained estimates of the proportion of males and females in each country's labor force from published census data collected as close to the time of each corresponding survey as possible. She then reweighted each sample to make the proportion of males and females in the labor force match the proportion in the census data. For example, an Austrian survey conducted in 1974 estimated that nation's labor force to be composed of 47 percent males and 53 percent females. In 1971, the nearest year for which statistics were available, corresponding census figures showed proportions of .61 and .39 for males and females, respectively. Using that information, the data were weighted by the ratio of expected (census) to obtained (survey) results. This procedure leaves unchanged the total sample size for each survey.

Roos proceeded to test how closely the weighted survey data matched census estimates of the age and occupational distributions of the male and female labor force. She computed an index of dissimilarity for each country and compared the distributions of age and occupation from each weighted survey with those of the census (taken from the closest year available). The index gives the percentage of survey respondents who would have to be in a different age or occupational group in order for a survey distribution to equal its corresponding census distribution, thus providing some indication of the extent of differences between respondents and nonrespondents.

Changes or differences in how the target population is defined can also result in noncomparability between surveys. Martin (1983: 683) points out, for example, that the census definition of "housing units" has changed with each successive census from 1940 to 1970. Each new definition is an attempt to refine the rather ambiguous distinction between residential and transient quarters. Since the number of people involved in these definition changes is rather small, most statistics will scarcely be affected. However, estimates of phenomena that are concentrated in certain subgroups (such as "hotel residents") may be more than trivially altered (Martin, 1983: 685). Not only households but also respondents must be defined according to the same criteria across surveys for samples to be comparable. A well-known case of noncomparability is that of the variations over time in census designations of racial and ethnic categories. Glenn and Frisbie (1977) summarize the changes that the Census Bureau has made in the specification of Mexican-Americans.

A similar problem of noncomparability may arise with regard to the geographic bounds of the target population, not because definitional criteria have changed but because geographic boundaries have (see Glenn and Frisbie, 1977: 97-98). The borders of SMSAs, central cities, and census tracts are not invariant and may change from census to census as, for example, when cities annex outlying areas. Such changes could result in misleading estimates of such phenomena as metropolitan growth. The Census Bureau provides information about boundary changes in "comparability tables" and footnotes in its published volumes, but strict comparability may not always be possible.

Changes or differences in definitions of "eligible respondents" are another source of noncomparability between surveys. In more tractable instances, particular types of respondents may be included in one survey but not another. This problem can often be dealt with by truncating the sample and excluding the types of respondents not included in all surveys being compared. However, the analysis should be conducted using both the truncated and complete versions of the sample to see whether omitting respondents substantially alters the results. For example, Niemi and Westholm (1983) used three Swedish and three American surveys to compare the two nations on attitude stability. In the three consecutive Swedish surveys, the minimum age was 21, 20, and 18, and persons over 80 were not interviewed, while in the U.S. surveys, adults 18 and over were interviewed. Tests were run with the data to determine whether excluding respondents under 21 (and over 80 for the United States) affected the stability coefficients obtained. Since the difference was trivial, the samples were truncated so that only respondents between 21 and 80 years of age were included in the analysis. If differences in such a case are nontrivial, the analysis should be presented for both truncated and total samples.

Even having survey data with identical definitions of the target population and similar sampling and respondent selection procedures, however, does not ensure that true changes in attitudes and behavior will be detected if demographic change has occurred in the population. Younger cohorts in the United States, for example, are better educated and have different rates of labor force participation, fertility, mortality, migration, and so on. Population characteristics change as younger cohorts replace older cohorts and as new members enter through in-migration. Hence any observed change could result from cohort succession or immigration rather than from changes in respondents who were in the population at all points in time being compared (Martin, 1983). Such changes in population composition do not really damage sample comparability, but they must be controlled for in any analysis of trends. For example, Glenn (1977: 37) recommends that since intra-cohort change may vary by sex, and since males have higher mortality rates, cohort analyses should be performed separately for males and females.

A number of studies have documented that interviewer charac-teristics (especially race, sex, and age) have an effect on responses to survey questions (e.g., Schuman and Converse, 1971). For instance, black respondents are more likely to express anti-white sentiments to black than to white interviewers. Noncomparability of samples over time is a distinct possibility because of changes in race relations (e.g., less deference to whites by younger blacks), and because the composition of interviewing staffs has changed. Interviewing staffs have become older and predominantly female, and the proportion of black interviewers has increased markedly since the mid-1960s. Many survey organizations now attempt to match interviewers and respondents by race. As a consequence, in many cases in which trends for black respondents are being examined, the extent of true change may be obscured by changes in the composition of interviewing staff. Fischer (1974, reported in Martin, 1983) analyzed the effects of an experimental manipulation in which black and white interviewers were randomly assigned to blocks estimated to be at least 15 percent black. The analysis compared data on anomia with baseline data on the topic gathered years earlier by white interviewers. The extent of observed change in anomia and relationships between anomia and age varied according to whether the interviewer was black or white. Based on these findings, Fischer concluded that, if possible, it is better to control race of interviewer when making comparisons over time among black respondents—for example, by limiting comparisons to blacks interviewed by whites (or blacks) at all points in time.

Whether interviews are conducted by telephone or in person can also affect the content of responses obtained. From the many studies that have been conducted (summarized in Martin, 1983), it appears that interviewing method affects reporting on different sorts of items in different ways (Groves and Kahn, 1979). Telephone surveys yield higher rates of missing data, less complete reporting, especially when detailed information is required, and more error in the information reported. However, telephone interviewing does not seem to increase socially desirable responses. Although respondents report feeling more uneasy about answering sensitive questions, they sometimes have been found to provide more information on the telephone than in person on sensitive topics such as alcohol use.

Whenever surveys conducted by different survey organizations ("houses") are to be compared or pooled, researchers should check for "house effects"—that is, interhouse differences in item marginals or trends that result from sampling procedures and interviewer training. House effects may be especially problematic when charting trends, as it may be impossible to distinguish time effects from house effects (Smith, 1978). To test for house effects on marginals, researchers should make interhouse comparisons of corresponding items from surveys conducted at approximately the same time. Smith (1978) limits comparisons to surveys spaced no more than five months apart. The most frequently observed presumed house effect to watch for is a difference in the proportion of "Don't know's" on attitude questions. For instance, the level of "Don't know's" on the General Social Survey has been found to be lower than that on the Roper poll (Smith, 1978) and the National Election Study (Smith, 1982). The difference has been attributed to methods of interviewer training; NORC interviewers are less likely to acknowledge nonattitudes. Differences in marginal distributions that remain after DKs are excluded may result from true change occurring between surveys because of intervening events, from response effects such as those due to variation in context (i.e., item order), or from residual contamination by nonattitude holders who nevertheless profess an opinion (Smith, 1982).

Smith (1978) presents examples of how to use t-tests of differences in proportions to test for house effects. We present a similar but hypothetical example. Suppose respondents in two surveys were asked to rate nations on a scale from −5 to +5, and the following proportions of respondents rated Andorra either a +3, +4, or +5:

Date	House	Pro-portion	N	Sig. of Diff.	Differ-ence	Prop. DK	Prop. with DKs Out	Sig. of Diff. with DKs Out
1/82	A	.507	1528	p = .03	−.055	.11	.570	N.S.
2/82	B	.562	1488			.06	.598	

When the DKs are excluded, the difference in proportions is no longer significant.

Researchers who are using data from different survey organizations for a trend analysis would also be wise to make an interhouse comparison of trends on each item (Smith, 1978). The general procedure is as follows: First, constant or no-change models are fitted to each house series. If these are inconsistent with observed trends, then linear change models are fitted. These may reveal a linear trend, a linear trend with unexplained variation, or no significant linear trend. Next, the trends found for each house time series are compared. A lack of sufficient overlapping data points to form corresponding series—for example, having three data points from one house and two from another—is likely to be a problem necessitating a considered judgment as to whether trends really are dissimilar. A two-point series can only be constant or linear, while a three-point or more series can be nonlinear as well. In such cases, one could test whether a nonlinear trend on the three-point series differs significantly from a constant or linear trend from the two-point series. Smith (1978) provides an example of an interhouse comparison of trends, and Taylor (1976) describes the statistical tests involved. Even apparent house differences in trends, however, may instead result from short-term fluctuations that are characteristic of many attitudes or from question-order effects (Smith, 1978).

Besides differences in marginal distributions and trends, other possible house effects may be investigated by examining differences in sample composition, bivariate correlations between attitude scales and demographics, and bivariate correlations among attitude items. For example, a comparison of the General Social Survey and the National Election Study revealed the first two types of interhouse differences to be negligible but demonstrated between-house variation in bivariate correlations between attitudes (Smith, 1982). In summary, while house effects are not a major problem, they exist and should be checked whenever surveys from different organizations are being used.

A final problem of sample comparability occurs in comparative longitudinal designs when the time period between surveys differs for the entities, as when countries are being compared. Under such circumstances, researchers should try to estimate what the results would have been if the time between waves were equal and encompassed the same years, perhaps by bringing in additional data. For example, in investigating attitude stability in Sweden and the United States, Niemi and Westholm (1983) used Swedish panel data spanning a three-year period from 1973 to 1976 and U.S. data over a four-year period from 1972 to 1976. They found greater attitude stability in Sweden but questioned whether it was due to the shorter time between waves. Fortunately, data for the United States were available for the two-year midpoint in 1974. Their strategy was to compare average stability coefficients for the 1972-1974 period and the 1974-1976 period with those for the four-year interval. Since the coefficients for the 1972-1974 period averaged .03 higher than those for the 1972-1976 period, the authors estimated that the U.S. stability coefficients would have increased by no more than .03 if the re-interviewing had occurred after three instead of four years.

The Problem of Sampling Error

Tests of significance generated by computer package programs such as SPSS[x] assume simple random sampling, an assumption that is never met. National surveys used quota control sampling until the mid-1950s and now use either modified probability or full probability sampling with a multistage cluster design.[6] Quota control samples selected certain segments of the population in some predetermined proportion based on census data (for example, certain proportions of males and females, or persons in a given age range). This procedure promoted representativeness on the quota control variables but not on uncontrolled variables such as education. Bias was introduced because interviewers had the freedom to select any respondents who were "demographically correct." The result was that interviewers tended to select accessible respondents residing within a small geographic area. The use of significance tests with quota control samples is problematic, since such samples are not random at any stage. For researchers who wish to apply significance tests, however, empirical study of the sampling variability of quota control samples (Stephan and McCarthy, 1958) has led to a rule of thumb that standard errors should be estimated at about 1.5 times those for simple random samples of the same size.[7]

"Modified probability" or "full probability" samples with a multistage cluster design are now used by survey organizations for face-to-face interviewing (see Kalton, 1983, for a detailed discussion of these sampling methods). In both modified and full probability samples of the United States, the nation is partitioned into a number of primary sampling units (PSUs), each comprised of a Standard Metropolitan

Statistical Area (SMSA) or a more rural area with a population the size of a small SMSA. The PSUs are then divided into smaller units, most often city blocks in urban areas or units of comparable size in more rural areas. In full probability sampling, a sample of households is drawn randomly from these smaller units, and when the individual is the unit of analysis, respondents are selected randomly from households. In modified probability sampling, quota sampling is used to select respondents, but unlike "quota control" sampling, interviewers must select respondents using a set procedure rather than their own discretion. Polls conducted by commercial survey organizations most often use modified probability sampling, while most academic survey organizations use full probability sampling.

Both modified and full probability samples require that a correction factor be applied to the standard error of estimate. Respondents within clusters tend to be somewhat homogeneous on variables that are related to residential segregation, such as occupational prestige, race, and income. The higher the correlation of a variable with the sample cluster, the greater its standard error will be. Variables such as sex and age, which are fairly evenly distributed across clusters, will have standard errors of about 1.1 or 1.15 times those for a random sample, while variables such as urban-rural residence, which are virtually constant for respondents within a cluster, may have a standard error four times that for a simple random sample of the same size (Glenn, 1975).

An accepted convention to adjust for this "cluster effect" has been to multiply the standard error generated for a random sample by a correction factor of 1.25 or 1.3. An alternative strategy suggested by the NORC is to apply to standard error obtained but to assume that the sample is two-thirds its size. Today, however, computer programs to calculate standard errors of estimates obtained from a complex sample design are increasingly available. Most typically these programs use one of three techniques: the Taylor expansion or delta method, the method of balanced repeated replications (BRR), or the "jack-knife" method (discussed in Kalton, 1983). By assuming that clusters are sampled with replacement, they slightly overestimate variance but have the advantage that the standard error formula for a given estimator remains the same, regardless of the sampling method used with PSUs. As a result, all that is required to use these programs is a variable denoting PSU and information about first-stage sampling procedures (Kalton, 1983). These techniques may become available through standard statistical package programs.

Standard errors may also be larger than under simple random sampling when telephone surveys are conducted. Two sampling methods frequently used are simple RDD (random digit dialing) and the Waksberg method, a two-stage, clustered probability-proportional-to-size RDD sampling design (see Kalton, 1983). Sampling error is increased in a simple RDD design because the number of working numbers per three-digit central office code is a random variable, and in the Waksberg method because clustering within telephone banks is used in the design. Groves (1978) has computed "defts" for attitudinal and demographic variables for these two sampling designs. A deft is the ratio of the actual standard error to the standard error of a simple random sample of the same size and is equal to the square root of the design effect. For the RDD sample Groves reports defts of between 1.04 for demographic variables and 1.07 for attitudinal variables. When the Wakesberg method is used, mean defts for attitudinal variables are 1.17, and mean defts for demographic variables are 1.42. Researchers should therefore inflate sampling variability accordingly when estimating sampling error from telephone surveys that use the Waksberg method.

Significance Tests with Multiple Surveys

Two alternate strategies that afford researchers greater confidence in their results by decreasing the probability of Type II errors are to increase the sample size or to perform replications on independent samples. Although the most common strategy in survey research is to increase the sample size by pooling surveys when a phenomenon under investigation has no temporal dimension, the individual surveys involved may also be treated as replications. A variety of methods have been developed for computing the statistical significance of an array of parameter estimates from a number of replications. These methods of testing for significance have most frequently been applied in psychology and education as means of summarizing the results of published studies of the same phenomenon under the label "meta-analysis," as discussed in Chapter 1 (see also Glass, 1978; Rosenthal, 1984; Rosenthal and Hall, 1981). These methods are also suited to social survey data analysis.

One of the most straightforward techniques for computing the statistical significance of parameter estimates from survey replications is the Stouffer method. Applying the method requires that one first convert the parameter estimates or test statistics from individual surveys to Z-values. Rosenthal and Hall (1981) discuss how to obtain equivalent values of Z for test statistics (such as t, F, or χ^2) and for estimates of effect size (e.g., r, phi, or d). Once Z values for the series of replications are computed, the next step is to take their mean $(\overline{Z})$. An overall level of significance for the combined probability, or the combined Z, is then calculated by multiplying the mean Z $(\overline{Z})$ by the square root of the number of replications. However, it is the mean Z $(\overline{Z})$ that is applied to a table of critical values such as that provided by Rosenthal and Hall (1981).

Below is an example of the Stouffer method using data from the General Social Surveys. Table 4 shows the zero-order correlations between respondents' reported happiness and the number of institutions in which they have little confidence. The t-ratio for each zero-order correlation was transformed to Z using the following formula (Rosenthal and Hall, 1981: 2):

$$Z = t(1 - (t^2/(4df)))$$

The mean Z $(\overline{Z})$ for the seven studies is 2.44. Since the mean Z for seven studies must be 1.97 to reach significance at the .0000001 level, the combined probability is highly significant. However, the low probability is a function of the large sample sizes. The correlations between confidence in institutions and happiness are very small, and therefore the implications should not be exaggerated.

Techniques for Studying Small Populations

Secondary analysis of pooled surveys is perhaps the most frequently used technique for studying small populations. Reed (1975-1976) provides a detailed discussion, using as an illustration a sample of southern Jews he constructed by pooling 56 Gallup surveys. A pooling design reduces sampling error by increasing the sample size and, when samples are independent (i.e., when they are drawn from sampling frames containing different PSUs), by augmenting the number of sampled PSUs. However, when sample designs contain a nonprobability component, as many surveys do at the block level, sampling error of the individual sample proportions cannot be estimated with any precision. Therefore, even the sampling error of the pooled proportion should be assumed to be at least twice that for a random sample.

TABLE 4
Zero-Order Correlations Between Number of Institutions
in Which Respondents Have Little Confidence
and Their Reported Happiness

Data File (N)	r	Z^a
1973-1980		
Pooled (8424)	−.086	Not computed
1973 (1203)	−.141	4.01
1974 (1223)	−.086	2.46
1975 (1162)	−.092	2.29
1976 (1119)	−.084	2.54
1977 (1284)	−.078	2.29
1978 (1249)	−.059	1.70
1980 (1184)	−.064	1.81
1973-1980 Mean	−.086	2.44 $p < .0000001$

SOURCE: General Social Surveys conducted by the National Opinion Research Center.
a. Zs were computed using a conservative assumption that each sample was two-thirds its size.

When samples are not independent, the critical issue is whether they are representative. When an independent estimate of the size of the rare population is available, it is possible to compare the proportion of the rare group in the pooled sample to its proportion in the independent estimate. Either overestimation or underestimation of the rare population in the pooled sample indicates that the sample is likely to be unrepresentative. If a group is clustered geographically, underrepresentation is likely to mean that the sample PSUs do not contain the group's population centers, while overrepresentation can mean that more isolated members have been overlooked. Comparing geographic location and size of place of the pooled sample with an independent sample can also give some indication of the representativeness of the sample of PSUs. For example, when Reed compared his pooled sample of southern Jews with an independent sample of the American Jewish Committee, he found a slight underrepresentation of the group in the pooled sample, mostly because the large cities of Florida were under-represented.

Overestimation of a small population can also mean that classification errors have occurred in which nonmembers of the rare population have been incorrectly labeled as members. When no independent estimates of the rare population are available, researchers must rely only on estimates from the pooled surveys. Researchers can take comfort from remembering that a group is not usually defined by a lone, dichotomous variable, which reduces the likelihood that a classification error will involve the category of interest. Many rare groups are defined by multiple characteristics such as region, ethnicity, and religious preference, and these variables often have several response categories. The greater the number of response categories of a defining characteristic (e.g., race), the smaller the likelihood that a misclassification will involve the group of interest. For example, Nelsen and Dickson's (1972) estimate of black Catholics obtained by pooling 28 Gallup surveys would be unaffected by Jews being mislabeled as having no religious preference. Finally, some of the group's defining characteristics can be cross-checked against other variables; for instance, a region can be cross-tabulated by PSU, and respondents who have been misclassified can be deleted from the sample. (The opposite problem, loss of members due to misclassification, should be negligible if the level of error is reasonable.)

State or other subnational populations are another sort of group that is small in number in national sample surveys. A method of estimating phenomena such as attitudes and voting in these groups is computer simulation (Pool et al., 1965; Weber et al., 1972-1973). This method proceeds in three stages. First, a model is constructed that best fits an actual set of survey data. Second, the validity of the model is retested by comparing estimates from the model with additional actual data from the surveys. Third, the model is used to estimate opinions on which data are not available. The technique assumes that attitudes and voting (or other dependent variables of interest) are determined by demographic and socioeconomic characteristics.

Weber et al. (1972-1973) used this method to estimate policy preferences for the 50 states. First, the electorate was partitioned into a number of "voter types" defined by region, size of place, occupation, age, sex, ethnicity, and religion. Information on the distribution of these voter types by state was obtained from census data. Synthetic electorates were created by estimating the voting preferences of each voter type. To do this, deviation scores for each demographic subgroup were calculated by subtracting that group's survey preference norm (e.g., the percentage voting for a Democratic candidate) from the national preference norm. Deviation scores for each demographic subgroup of which a voter type was a member were then summed and added to the national preference norm. Pearson correlations and other statistics were used to evaluate the fit between actual and simulated voting percentages across several surveys using different methods of estimation. The method that provided the best fit was further validated by applying it to estimate the level of education in the same surveys. Finally, policy preferences by state were estimated by obtaining the distribution of preferences for the demographic subgroups used to define the voter types and then calculating preferences by voter type and synthetic electorates as before (see Weber et al., 1972-1973, for details).

These opportunities and caveats for making effective use of existing survey data are by no means exhaustive. The reader should consult the references cited in each section for more detailed discussions of the variety of research designs to which secondary analysis can be applied, problems of item and sample comparability, and statistical issues and options to consider when using existing surveys. The secondary analyst must also deal with the problems that are a part of all survey analysis. Most of the difficulties inherent in secondary analysis, however, may be handled satisfactorily and are far outweighed by the opportunities for research using preexisting data.

4. CONCLUSION

Secondary survey analysis, or the use of precollected survey data in original research, has claimed a central position in social scientific inquiry. Secondary analysis affords investigators the opportunity to complete research projects economically with respect to both money and time. The preparation and storage of a wide variety of machine-readable data files in social science data archives have increased the availability of data. Familiarity with data archives and existing data sets will facilitate the research process, and researchers will be better able to evaluate the types of hypotheses that can be tested through secondary analysis. Moreover, knowledge of existing data sets often sparks ideas for additional research.

While the potential of secondary analysis is tremendous, certain pitfalls are to be avoided. Perhaps the biggest temptation is to formulate questions solely because a particular data set is available. Although this seems similar to generating hypotheses based on one's knowledge of available data, the process is radically different. Overriding theoretical

76

orientations and large research questions need to be a guiding force rather than a byproduct of research.

Researchers seeking survey data should keep in mind that all organizations with precollected social survey data can be thought of as data storehouses. Government agencies, private foundations, charitable organizations, and firms in private industry all potentially offer resources that complement those of academic archives. Consulting academic archives is generally a good first step, however, for archivists typically know which data files are available for studying a specific problem and how to acquire them.

Although existing surveys provide countless possibilities for research, these data (like the social world we study) are often far from perfect. As researchers, we must be aware of data set limitations and do the best we can with what is available (Hyman, 1972: 281). Often this requires working with several data sets simultaneously. Besides expert knowledge of research designs and statistical techniques, an open mind and a measure of creativity are invaluable assets for doing secondary analysis.

APPENDIX A: U.S. SOCIAL SCIENCE DATA ARCHIVES

California
Data Archives Library
Institute for Social Science Research
University of California
Los Angeles, CA 90024
(213) 825-0716

Project Talent Data Bank
American Institutes for Research
P.O. Box 1113, 1791 Arastradero Road
Palo Alto, CA 94302
(415) 493-3550

The Rand Corporation
Computer Services Department Data
  Facility
1700 Main Street
Santa Monica, CA 90406
(213) 393-0411 Ext. 7351

State Data Program
University of California at Berkeley
2538 Channing Way
Berkeley, CA 94720
(415) 642-6571

Connecticut
Social Science Data Archive
Social Science Library
Box 1958, Yale Station
New Haven, CT 06520
(203) 436-4771

The Roper Center for Public Opinion
  Research
User Services
The University of Connecticut
Box U-164
Storrs, CT 06268
(203) 486-4440

Florida
Department of Reference
University of Florida Libraries
Gainesville, FL 32611
(904) 392-0363

Illinois
National Opinion Research Center
University of Chicago
1155 E. 60th St.
Chicago, IL 60637
(312) 962-1213

Data Services
Vogelback Computing Center
Northwestern University
Evanston, IL 60201
(312) 492-3691

Indiana
Indiana Political Data Archive and
  Laboratory
Department of Political Science
215 Woodburn Hall
Indiana University
Bloomington, IN 47405
(812) 335-6361

Iowa
Laboratory for Political Research
345 Schaeffer Hall
The University of Iowa
Iowa City, IA 52242
(319) 353-3033

Maryland
National Center for Health Statistics
3700 East-West Highway
Hyattsville, MD 20782
(301) 436-8500

Massachusetts
The Henry A. Murray Research Center of
  Radcliffe College
10 Garden Street
Cambridge, MA 02138
(617) 495-8140

Michigan
Inter-University Consortium for Political
  & Social Research (ICPSR)
Institute for Social Research
P.O. Box 1248
Ann Arbor, MI 48106
(313) 763-5010

Montana
Center for Data Systems and Analysis
Montana State University
24 E. Renne Library
Bozeman, MT 59717
(406) 994-4481

New Jersey
CCIS-Hill Center
Busch Campus, P.O. Box 579
Rutgers University
Piscataway, NJ 08854
(201) 932-2483

Social Science User Service
Princeton University Computer Center
87 Prospect Avenue
Princeton, NJ 08544
(609) 452-6052

New York
Center for Social Analysis
State University of New York
Binghamton, NY 13901
(607) 798-2116

Center for the Social Sciences
Columbia University
420 W. 118th Street
New York, NY 10027
(212) 280-3038

CISER (Cornell Institute for Social and
  Economic Research)
Cornell University
323 Uris Hall
Ithaca, NY 14853
(607) 256-4801

Library Information Service
Baruch College
City College of New York
156 E. 25th Street
New York, NY 10010
(202) 725-7135/725-7114

North Carolina
Louis Harris Data Center (and)
Social Science Data Library
Institute for Research in Social Science
Room 10 Manning Hall 026A
University of North Carolina
Chapel Hill, NC 27514
(919) 966-3346

Ohio
Institute for Policy Research
The University of Cincinnati
Cincinnati, OH 45221
(513) 475-5028

Polimetrics Laboratory
Ohio State University
Department of Political Science
145 Derby Hall, 154 No. Oval Mall
Columbus, OH 43210
(614) 422-1061

Oklahoma
Oklahoma Data Archive
Center for the Application of the Social
    Sciences
Oklahoma State University
Stillwater, OK 74074
(405) 624-5641

Pennsylvania
Social Science Computer Research
    Institute
University of Pittsburgh
5R01 Forbes Quad
Pittsburgh, PA 15260
(412) 624-5559

Social Science Data Center
390 McNeil Bldg. CR
3718 Locust Walk
University of Pennsylvania
Philadelphia, PA 19104
(215) 898-6454

Texas
Drug Abuse Epidemiology Data Center
(DAEDAC)
Behavioral Research Program
Texas A&M University
College Station, TX 77843
(409) 845-0380

Virginia
Data Use & Access Laboratories
(DUALLABS)
1515 Wilson Boulevard
Arlington, VA 22209
(703) 525-1480

National Technical Information Service
5285 Port Royal Road
Springfield, VA 22161
(703) 487-4763

Washington
Center for Social Science Computation
    and Research
University of Washington
145 Savery Hall, DK-45
Seattle, WA 98195
(206) 543-8110

Washington, D.C.
Data User Services Division
Customer Services Branch
Bureau of the Census
Washington, DC 20233
(202) 763-4100

Machine Readable Records Branch
(NNSR)
National Archives & Records
    Administration
Washington, DC 20408
(202) 523-3267

Wisconsin
Data and Program Library Service
University of Wisconsin
Social Science Building, Rm. 3313
Madison, WI 53706
(608) 262-7962

APPENDIX B: SOCIAL SCIENCE DATA ARCHIVES OUTSIDE THE UNITED STATES

Amsterdam
Steinmetz Archives
Herengracht 410-412
1017 BX Amsterdam
(020) 225061

Australia
Sample Survey Centre
University of Sydney
Sydney, New South Wales
Australia 2006
(02) 692-3624, 692-3623

Social Science Data Archives
Australian National University
G.P.O. Box 4, Canberra 2601

Belgium
Belgian Archives for the Social Sciences
Place Montesquieu, 1 Boite 18
B-1348 Louvain-la-Neuve, Belgium
(010) 41-81-81, Ext. 4272

Canada
Data Library and Computing Centre
The University of British Columbia
6356 Agricultural Road
University Campus
Vancouver, British Columbia
Canada V6T 1W5
(604) 228-5587

Institute for Behavioral Research
York University
4700 Keele Street
Downsview, Ontario
Canada M3J 2R6
(416) 667-3022, 667-3026, 667-3721

Leisure Studies Data Bank
Department of Recreation
University of Waterloo
Waterloo, Ontario
Canada N2L 3G1
(519) 885-1211

Public Archives Canada
395 Wellington Street
Ottawa, Ontario
Canada, K1A 0N3
(613) 593-7772

Social Science Data Library
Department of Sociology
Carleton University
Ottawa, Ontario
Canada K1S 5B6
(613) 231-6650

Chile
Celade Latin America Population Data
    Bank
United Nations Latin American
    Demographic Center
Avenida Dag Hammarskjold
Casilla 91
Santiago, Chile
Cables: UNDEM

Denmark
Danish Data Archives
Odense University
Niels Bohrs Alle 25
DK-5230 Odense M
(09) 15-86-00, 15-79-20

England
International Statistical Institute
35-37 Grosvenor Gardens
London, SW1W OBS
(01) 828-4242

Social Science Research Council Data
    Archive (SSRC)
University of Essex
Wivenhoe Park
Colchester CO4 3SQ
Essex, England
(44) 206-860570, 206-862286

France
Banque de Donnees Socio-Politiques
Universite des Science Sociales de
    Grenoble
C.E.R.A.T., B.P. 34
F-38401 Saint Martin d'Heres

India
Indian Council of Social Science
    Research
35 Ferozshah Road
New Delhi-11011

Italy
Archivio Dati e Programmi per le
    Scienze Sociali
Instituti Superiori di Sociologica
Via G. Cantoni 4
I-20144 Milan

Norway
Norwegian Social Science Data
    Services
Universitetet i Bergen
Hans Holmboesgate 22
N-5014 Bergen

Poland
Polska Akademia Nauk
Wydzial I Nauk Spolecznych
Komitet Nauk-Politzcznych
Skrytka Pocztowa 12
PL-00-504 Warsaw

Senegal
Universitye De Dakar
Ecole Des Bibliothexaires
Boite Postale 3252 Dakar
(221) 230739

Sweden
Karolinska Institute Library and
    Information Center
P.O.Box 60201
S-104-01 Stockholm
(46) 8-23-22-70

Swedish Social Science Data Service
Box 5048
S-402-21 Goteborg
(031) 63-10-00 Ext. 1207

West Germany
Zentralarchiv für Empirische
    Sozialforschung
Universität zu Köln
Bachemer Str. 40
Köln 41, West Germany
D-5000
(0221) 44-40-86

NOTES

1. Most social research methods texts include discussions of how to conduct content analyses (see, e.g., Bailey, 1982). See Lantz et al. (1975) for an example of historical content analysis that tackles the difficulties inherent in quantifying data contained in documents.

2. Glenn, personal communication.

3. Archives were included in Table 1 only if a significant proportion of their holdings are available to the general public, and if the majority of them are of more than regional interest.

4. Principal investigators of the National Election Study surveys have varied.

5. Wright et al. (1982) later elaborated this typology of the American class structure and conducted a primary survey that enabled them to formulate precise indicators of the dimensions of social class.

6. This discussion is taken from Glenn (1975, 1977).

7. Another problem of using significance tests from the 1930s and 1940s is that the samples were designed to be representative of the voting population. Not until the late 1950s and 1960s did they become fully representative. Glenn (1977) illustrates a method of standardization to adjust estimates of percentages for groups such as southerners, who are underrepresented. Percentages based on a small number of respondents have considerable sampling variability. Using standardization to increase the contribution of a small group to the percentage estimate for the total population increases the sampling variability of the percentage estimate for the total sample. Glenn (1977) suggests that to compensate, when estimating the difference between an adjusted percentage and an unadjusted one, one should increase the difference required for significance by 15 percent. When two adjusted percentages are being compared, the difference between them required for significance should be increased by 30 percent.

REFERENCES

ACOCK, A., H. D. CLARKE, and M. C. STEWART (1985) "A new model for old measures: A covariance structure analysis of political efficacy." Journal of Politics 47, 4.

ALLISON, P. D. (1984) Event History Analysis: Regression for Longitudinal Event Data. Sage University Papers 46: Quantitative Applications in the Social Sciences.

American Demographics (1980) A Researcher's Guide to the 1980 Census. Ithaca, NY: American Demographics.

BAILEY, K. D. (1982) Methods of Social Research. New York: Free Press.

BIELBY, W. T., C. B. HAWLEY, and D. BILLS (1979) Research Uses of the National Longitudinal Surveys. Washington, DC: U.S. Dept. of Labor R & D Monograph No. 62.

BISHOP, G. F., R. W. OLDENDICK, A. J. TUCHFARBER, and S. E. BENNETT (1979) "Effects of opinion filtering and opinion floating: Evidence from a secondary analysis." Political Methodology 6(3): 293-309.

BLALOCK, H. M. (1984) "Contextual-effects models: Theoretical and methodological issues." Annual Review of Sociology 10: 353-372.

CAMPBELL, A., P. E. CONVERSE, W. E. MILLER, and D. STOKES (1960) The American Voter. New York: John Wiley.

Center for Human Resource Research (1982) The National Longitudinal Surveys Handbook. Columbus: Ohio State University.

CURTIN, R. T. (1982) "Indicators of consumer behavior: The University of Michigan surveys of consumers." Public Opinion Quarterly 46 (Spring): 340-352.

DAVIS, J. A. (1983) General Social Surveys, 1972-1983 [machine-readable data file]. Chicago: National Opinion Research Center. [producer]. Roper Public Opinion Center [distributor].

DAYMONT, T. N. and P. J. ANDRISANI (1983) "The research uses of the National Longitudinal Surveys: An update." Review of Public Data Use 11: 203-310.

de GUCHTENEIRE, P., L. Le DUC, and R. G. NIEMI (1985) "A compendium of academic survey studies of elections around the world." Electoral Studies 4: 167-182.

Economic Behavior Program (1953-1976) Surveys of Consumers [machine-readable data files]. Ann Arbor, MI: Survey Research Center. [producer]. ICPSR [distributor].

ELDER, G. H., Jr. [ed.] (1985) Life Course Dynamics: Trajectories and Transitions. Ithaca, NY: Cornell University Press.

———(1974) Children of the Great Depression. Chicago: University of Chicago Press.

ENGELBERG, L. (1981) "Towards a sex-class theory of stratification: An analysis of health care workers in contemporary capitalism." Unpublished Ph.D. dissertation, University of California at Los Angeles.

FISCHER, E. M. (1974) "Change in anomie in Detroit from the 1950's to 1971." Unpublished Ph.D. dissertation, the University of Michigan, Ann Arbor.

GEDA, C. L. (1978) "Social science data archives." Presented at the annual meetings of the Society of American Archivists, Nashville.

GLASS, G. V (1978) "Integrated findings: The meta-analysis of research." Review of Research in Education 5: 351-379.

GLENN, N. D. (1980) "Values, attitudes, and beliefs," pp. 596-640 in O. G. Brim, Jr. and J. Kagan (eds.) Constancy and Change in Human Development. Cambridge, MA: Harvard University Press.

———(1977) Cohort Analysis. Sage University Papers 5: Quantitative Applications in the Social Sciences.

———(1975) "Trend studies with available survey data: Opportunities and pitfalls," pp. 6-48 in J. Southwick and P. Hastings, Survey Data for Trend Analysis: An Index to Repeated Questions in U.S. National Surveys Held by the Roper Public Opinion Research Center. Williamstown, MA: Roper Center.

———and W. P. FRISBIE (1977) "Trend studies with survey sample and census data." Annual Review of Sociology 3: 79-104.

GLENN, N. and C. WEAVER (1982) "Enjoyment of work by full-time workers in the U.S., 1955 and 1980." Public Opinion Quarterly 46 (Winter): 459-470.

GLENN N., P. E. CONVERSE, S. J. CUTLER, and H. H. HYMAN (1978) "The general social surveys." Contemporary Sociology 7(5): 532-549.

GROVES, R. M. (1978) "An empirical comparison of two telephone sample designs." Journal of Marketing Research 15: 622-631.

———and R. KAHN (1979) Surveys by Telephone: A National Comparison with Personal Interviews. New York: Academic Press.

HOUSE, J. S. (1979) "The University of Michigan election surveys as a data resource for sociologists." Contemporary Sociology 8: 46-53.

HYMAN, H. H. (1972) Secondary Analysis of Sample Surveys: Principles, Procedures, and Potentialities. New York: John Wiley.

Institute for Research in Social Science (1981) Directory of Louis Harris Public Opinion Machine-Readable Data. Chapel Hill, NC: Author.

Inter-University Consortium of Political and Social Research (1984) Guide to Resources and Services, 1984-1985. Ann Arbor: University of Michigan.

KALTON, G. (1983) Introduction to Survey Sampling. Sage University Papers 35: Quantitative Applications in the Social Sciences.

KAPLAN, C. P., T. Van VALEY, et al. (1980) Census '80: Continuing the Fact-Finder Tradition. Washington, DC: Bureau of the Census.

KATONA, G. (1975) Psychological Economics. New York: Elsevier.

KESSLER, R. C. and D. F. GREENBERG (1981) Linear Panel Analysis: Models of Quantitative Change. New York: Academic Press.

LANTZ, H., J. KEYES, and M. SCHULTZ (1975) "The family in the preindustrial period: From base lines in history to change." American Sociological Review 40 (February): 21-36.

LONG, J. S. (1983a) Confirmatory Factor Analysis. Sage University Papers 33: Quantitative Applications in the Social Sciences.

———(1983b) Covariance Structure Models. Sage University Papers 34: Quantitative Applications in the Social Sciences.

MARTIN, E. (1983) "Surveys as social indicators: Problems in monitoring trends," pp. 677-743 in P. H. Rossi et al. (eds.) Handbook of Survey Research. New York: Academic Press.

————D. McDUFFEE, and S. PRESSER (1981) Sourcebook of Harris National Surveys: Repeated Questions 1963-1976. Chapel Hill, NC: Institute for Research in Social Science.

MIGDAL, S., R. ABELES, and L. SHERROD (1981) An Inventory of Longitudinal Studies of Middle and Old Age. New York: Social Science Research Council.

MILLER, W. E. and A. H. MILLER (1976) American National Election Study, 1976 [machine-readable data file]. Ann Arbor: Center for Political Studies. [producer]. ICPSR [distributor].

————et al. (1972) American National Election Study, 1972 [machine-readable data file]. Ann Arbor: Center for Political Studies. [producer]. ICPSR [distributor].

MORGAN, J. N. (1980) Panel Study of Income Dynamics, 1968-1980 [machine-readable data file]. Ann Arbor: Economic Behavior Program [producer]. ICPSR [distributor].

————and the staff of the Economic Behavior Program (1974-1983) Five Thousand American Families—Patterns of Economic Progress. (Volumes 1-10). Ann Arbor: Institute for Social Research.

MOTT, F. L., R. J. HAURIN, and W. MARSIGLIO (1983) "The impact of longitudinal data files on research on women's roles." Presented at the annual meetings of the American Sociological Association, Detroit.

MULLNER, R. M., C. S. BYRE, and C. L. KILLINGSWORTH (1983) "An inventory of U.S. health care data bases." Review of Public Data Use 11: 85-192.

National Center for Education Statistics (1981) NCES Directory of Computer Data Tapes. Washington, DC: Author.

National Center for Health Statistics (1970-1979) National Health Interview Surveys [machine-readable data files]. Hyattsville, MD: Author. [producer]. National Technical Information Service [distributor].

————(1971-75) National Health and Nutrition Examination Surveys [machine-readable data files]. Hyattsville, MD: Author. [producer]. National Technical Information Service [distributor].

NELSEN, H. M. and L. DICKSON (1972) "Attitudes of black Catholics and Protestants: Evidence for religious identity." Sociological Analysis 33 (Fall): 152-165.

NIEMI, R. G. and A. WESTHOLM (1983) "Issues, parties and attitudinal stability: A comparative study of Sweden and the United States." Presented at the workshop on "Over-Time Analysis," European Consortium for Political Research, Freiburg.

OSTROM, C. W., Jr. (1978) Time Series Analysis: Regression Techniques. Sage University Papers 9: Quantitative Applications in the Social Sciences.

PARNES, H. S. (1980) National Longitudinal Surveys of Labor Market Experience [machine-readable data file]. Columbus, OH: Center for Human Resource Research. [producer and distributor].

POOL, I. de Sola, R. P. ABELSON, and S. POPKIN (1965) Candidates, Issues, and Strategies: A Computer Simulation of the 1960 and 1964 Presidential Elections (rev. ed.). Cambridge: MIT Press.

POULANTZAS, N. (1975) Classes in Contemporary Capitalism. London: New Left.

PRESSER, S. (1982) "Studying social change with survey data: Examples from Louis Harris Surveys." Social Indicators Research 10: 407-422.

QUINN, R. P., T. W. MANGIONE, and S. E. SEASHORE (1973) Quality of Employment Survey, 1972-1973 [machine-readable data file]. Ann Arbor, MI: Institute for Social Research. [producer]. ICPSR [distributor].

QUINN, R. P., S. E. SEASHORE, and T. W. MANGIONE (1970) Survey of Working Conditions, 1969-1970 [machine-readable data file]. Ann Arbor, MI: Institute for Social Research. [producer]. ICPSR [distributor].

RABIER, J.-R. and R. INGLEHART (1975) Euro-Barometer 3: European Men and Women, May, 1975 [machine-readable data file]. Brussels: Commission of the European Communities [producer]. ICPSR [distributor].

REED, J. S. (1975-1976) "Needles in haystacks: Studying 'rare' populations by secondary analysis of national sample surveys." Public Opinion Quarterly 39(Winter): 514-522.

ROOS, P. A. (1985) Gender and Work: A Comparative Analysis of Industrial Societies. Albany: State University of New York Press.

The Roper Center (1984a) Data Acquisitions: January 1982-June 1984. Storrs, CT: Author.

———(1984b) The Roper Center American Collection. Storrs, CT: Author.

———(1982) A Guide to Roper Center Resources for the Study of American Race Relations. Storrs, CT: Author.

ROSENTHAL, R. (1984) Meta-Analytic Procedures for Social Research. Beverly Hills, CA: Sage.

———and J. HALL (1981) "Critical values of Z for combining independent probabilities." Replications in Social Psychology 1 (Winter): 1-6.

ROWE, J. S. (1973) "Using government data for research and instruction: The United States census as a paradigm." Proceedings of the ESOMAR/World Association of Public Opinion Research Congress, Budapest.

Royal Netherlands Academy of Arts and Sciences Social Science Information and Documentation Centre (1983) Steinmetz Archives Catalogue and Guide. Amsterdam: Author.

RUSK, J. G. (1982) "The Michigan election studies: A critical evaluation." Micropolitics 2 (2): 87-109.

SAS Institute (1982) SAS User's Guide: Basic. Cary, NC: Author.

SAYLES, M. (1983) "Alienation, social conflict, and relative deprivation: The roots of political activism." Unpublished Ph.D. dissertation, University of California at Los Angeles.

SCHUMAN, H. and J. CONVERSE (1971) "The effects of black and white interviewers on black responses in 1968." Public Opinion Quarterly 35: 44-68.

SCHUMAN, H. and S. PRESSER (1981) Questions and Answers in Attitude Surveys: Experiments on Question Form, Wording, and Context. New York: Academic Press.

SMITH, T. W. (1982) "House effects and the reproducibility of survey measurements: A comparison of the 1980 GSS and the 1980 American National Election Study." Public Opinion Quarterly 46 (Spring): 54-68.

———(1981a) Annotated Bibliography of Papers Using the General Social Surveys. Chicago: National Opinion Research Center.

———(1981b) "Happiness: Time trends, seasonal variations, intersurvey differences, and other mysteries." Social Psychology Quarterly 42(1): 18-30.

———1978 "In search of house effects: A comparison of responses to various questions by different survey organizations." Public Opinion Quarterly 42 (Winter): 533-543.

Social Science Research Council Survey Archive (n.d.) Abbreviated Guide to the Survey Archives Social Science Data Holdings. Essex: University of Essex.

———(n.d.) Guide to the Survey Archives Social Science Data Holdings and Allied Services. Essex: University of Essex.

SOUTHWICK, J. and P. HASTINGS (1975) Survey Data for Trend Analysis. Williamstown, MA: Roper Center.

Statistical Package for the Social Sciences (1983) SPSS^x User's Guide. New York: McGraw-Hill.

STEPHAN, F. F. and P. J. McCARTHY (1958) Sampling Opinions. New York: John Wiley.

STIPAK, B. and C. HENSLER (1982) "Statistical inferences in contextual analysis." American Journal of Political Science 26 (February): 151-175.

TAEUBER, R. C. and R. C. ROCKWELL (1982) "National social data series: A compendium of brief descriptions." Review of Public Data Use 10 (May): 23-111.

TAYLOR, D. G. (1976) "Procedures for evaluating trends in qualitative indicators," in J. A. Davis (ed.) Studies in Social Change Since 1948 (NORC Report 127A). Chicago: National Opinion Research Center.

———P. B. SHEATSLEY, and A. M. GREELEY (1978) "Attitudes toward racial integration." Scientific American 238 (June): 42-49.

TUMA, N. B. and M. T. HANNAN (1984) Social Dynamics: Models and Methods. New York: Academic Press.

———and L. P. GROENEVELD (1979) "Dynamic analysis of event-histories." American Journal of Sociology 4 (January): 820-854.

U.S. Department of Commerce (1983) Census of Population and Housing, 1980: Public Use Microdata Samples Technical Documentation. Washington, DC: Bureau of the Census.

———(1982) "Current Population Survey Overview." Data Development (August): 1-5.

———(1980) Bureau of the Census Catalogue, 1980. Washington, DC: Bureau of the Census.

———(1979) Directory of Data Files. Washington, DC: Bureau of the Census.

U.S. Department of Commerce, Bureau of the Census (1982) Current Population Survey: Annual Demographic File, 1982 [machine-readable data file]. Washington, DC: Author. [producer]. Data User Services Division [distributor].

———(1980a) Census of Population and Housing, 1980 [machine-readable data file] Washington, DC: Author. [producer]. Data User Services Division [distributor].

———(1980b) Questionnaire Reference Book. Washington, DC: Author.

U.S. Department of Commerce, Bureau of Economic Analysis (n.d.) Publications and Computer Tapes of the Bureau of Economic Analysis. Washington, DC: Author.

U.S. Department of Health and Health Services (1980) Catalog of Public Use Data Tapes From the National Center for Health Statistics. Hyattsville, MD: Author.

———(1981a) The 25th Anniversary of the National Health Survey. Hyattsville, MD: Author.

———(1981b) Data Systems of the National Center for Health Statistics. Hyattsville, MD: Author.

U.S. Department of Labor (1965) Dictionary of Occupational Titles (3rd ed.). Washington DC: U.S. Government Printing Office.

VANNEMAN, R. and F. C. PAMPEL (1977) "The American perception of class and status." American Sociological Review 42: 422-437.

VAVRA, J. K. (1981) "The Inter-University Consortium for Political and Social Research: A resource for the social scientist." Review of Public Data Use 9: 237-239.

VERDONIK, F. and L. SHERROD (1984) An Inventory of Longitudinal Research on Childhood and Adolescence. New York: Social Science Research Council.

87

WEBER, R. E., A. H. HOPKINS, M. L. MEZEY, and F. J. MUNGER (1972-1973) "Computer simulation of state electorates." Public Opinion Quarterly 36 (Winter): 549-565.

WRIGHT, E. O. and L. PERRONE (1977) "Marxist class categories and income inequality." American Sociological Review 42: 32-55.

WRIGHT, E. O., C. COSTELLO, D. HACHEN, and J. SPRAGUE (1982) "The American class structure." American Sociological Review 47 (December): 709-726.

K. JILL KIECOLT is Assistant Professor in the Department of Sociology at Louisiana State University. She received her Ph.D. from the University of California at Los Angeles. Her current research interests include the determinants of political and intergroup attitudes and the relationship of attitudes and social structure over time and across the life course. Her articles have appeared in such journals as the Public Opinion Quarterly, the Social Science Quarterly, and Environment and Behavior.

LAURA E. NATHAN is Assistant Professor of Sociology at Mills College and holds a Ph.D. from the University of California at Los Angeles. Her substantive areas of interest are medical sociology and social stratification, and her recent publications have focused on the psychosocial aspects of cancer and women in the male-dominated professions. Her current research addresses the impact of a cancer diagnosis on the family unit.

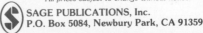

Quantitative Applications in the Social Sciences

(a Sage University Papers Series)

$6.00 each

SAGE PUBLICATIONS, INC.
P.O. BOX 5084
NEWBURY PARK, CALIFORNIA 91359

Place
Stamp
here

Quantitative Applications in the Social Sciences

A SAGE UNIVERSITY PAPERS SERIES

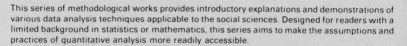

This series of methodological works provides introductory explanations and demonstrations of various data analysis techniques applicable to the social sciences. Designed for readers with a limited background in statistics or mathematics, this series aims to make the assumptions and practices of quantitative analysis more readily accessible.

SAGE PUBLICATIONS
The Publishers of Professional Social Science
Beverly Hills   Newbury Park   London   New Delhi